SARVEPALLI RADHAKRISHNAN, (1888-1975) is universally recognized as modern India's greatest philosopher. He was also a statesman of distinction, and even compared to Plato's ideal of the philosopher-king. As a creative thinker and a distinguished interpreter of Indian thought he philosophized in the true Indian tradition. His notion of religion was spiritual, and not institutional or denominational.

Born in the pilgrim soil of Tirutani (now in Andhra Pradesh), he imbibed lasting impression of India's Vedic heritage during his formative years. Starting with his first teaching appointment in the Department of Philosophy at Madras Presidency College in 1909, he quickly established his reputation, and in 1921 became George V Professor of Philosophy in Calcutta University and the Spalding Professor of Eastern Religion and Ethics at Oxford University in 1936. In 1952 he accepted the office of India's first Vice President, and in 1962 assumed the office of the President of India.

He was knighted in 1931 and conferred the *Bharat Ratna* Award in 1954.

LIVING WITH A PURPOSE

S. Radhakrishnan

Orient
Paperbacks

DELHI | MUMBAI | HYDERABAD

ISBN : 978-81-222-0031-7

Living With a Purpose: Turning Dreams into Reality

Subject: Literary Collections / Essays

© S. Gopal

1st Published 1977
15th Printing 2013

Published by
Orient Paperbacks
(A division of Vision Books Pvt. Ltd.)
5A/8, Ansari Road, New Delhi-110 002
www.orientpaperbacks.com

Cover design by Vision Studio

Printed at
Anand Sons, Delhi-110 092, India

Cover Printed at
Ravindra Printing Press, Delhi-110 006, India

CONTENTS

— ❧ —

The truly great are not the men of wealth, of possessions, not men who gain name and fame, but those who testify to the truth in them and refuse to compromise whatever be the cost. They are determined to do what they consider to be right. We may punish their bodies, refuse them comforts, but we connot buy their souls, we cannot break their spirits. Whoever possesses this invulnerability of spirit even to a little extent deserves our admiration.

S. Radhakrishnan

KALIDASA

— ৯ —

India's spirit, grace and genius.

Great classics of literature spring from profound depths in human experience. They come to us who live centuries later, in vastly different conditions, as the voice of our own experience. They release echoes within ourselves of what we never suspected was there. The deeper one goes into one's own experience, facing destiny, fighting fate, or enjoying love, the more does one's experience have in common with the experiences of others, in climes and ages. The most unique is the most universal. The Dialogues of the Buddha or of Plato, the dramas of Sophocles, the plays of Shakespeare, are both national and universal. The more profoundly they are rooted in historical traditions, the more uniquely do they know themselves and elicit powerful responses from others. There is a timeless and spaceless quality about great classics.

Kalidasa is the great representative of India's spirit, grace and genius. The Indian national consciousness is the base from which his works grow. Kalidasa has absorbed India's cultural heritage, made it his own, enriched it, given it universal scope and significance. Its spiritual directions, its intellectual amplitude, its artistic expressions, its political forms and economic arrangements, all find utterance in fresh, vital, shining phrases. We find in his works simple dignity of language, precision of phrase, classical taste, cultivated judgment, intense poetic sensibility and fusion of thought and feeling.

In his dramas we find pathos, power, beauty, and great skill in the construction of plot and delineation of character. He is at home in royal courts and on mountain tops, in happy homes and forest hermitages. He has a balanced outlook which enables him to deal sympathetically with men of high and low degree, fishermen, courtesans, servants. These great qualities make his works belong to the literature of the world. Humanity recognizes itself in them though they deal with Indian themes.

In India Kalidasa is recognized as the greatest poet and dramatist in Sanskrit literature. While once the poets were being counted, Kalidasa as being the first occupied the last finger. But the ring-finger remained true to its name, *anamika*, nameless, since the second to Kalidasa has not yet been found. Tradition associates Kalidasa with King Vikramaditya of Ujjayini, who founded the Vikrama era of 57 B.C. The change in the name of the hero of *Vikramorvasiya* from Pururavas to Vikrama lends support to the view that Kalidasa belonged to the court of King Vikramaditya of Ujjayini. Agnimitra who is the hero of the drama *Malavikagnimitra* was not a well-known monarch to deserve special notice by Kalidasa. He belonged to the second century Before Christ and his capital was Vidisa. Kalidasa's selection of this episode and his reference to Vidisa as the famous capital of a King in *Meghaduta* suggest that Kalidasa was a contemporary of Agnimitra. It is clear that Kalidasa flourished after Agnimitra (150 B.C) and before A.D 634, the date of the famous Aihole inscription which refers to Kalidasa as a great poet. If the suggestion that some verses of Mandas or inscription of A.D. 473 assume knowledge of Kalidasa's writings is accepted, then his date cannot be later than the end of the fourth century A.D. There are similarities between Asvaghosa's *Buddhacarita* and Kalidasa's works. If Asvaghosa is the debtor, then Kalidasa was of an earlier date than the first century A.D. If Kalidasa is the debtor, then his date would be later than the first century.

It is suggested that Kalidasa belongs to the Gupta period (A.D. 320-547) and lived in the reign of Chandragupta II, who had the title of Vikramaditya. He came to power about A.D. 345 and ruled till about A.D. 414. Whichever date we adopt, we are in the region of reasonable conjecture and nothing more.

Kalidasa speaks very little of himself and we cannot therefore be sure of his authorship of many works attributed to him. There is, however, general agreement about Kalidasa's authorship of the following works:

1. *Abhijnana-Sakuntala*, a drama in seven acts dealing with the love and marriage of Dusyanta and Sakuntala;

2. *Vikramorvasiya*, a drama in five acts dealing with the love and marriage of Pururavas and Urvasi;

3. *Malavikagnimitra*, a drama in five acts dealing with the love of Malavika and Agnimitra;

4. *Raghuvamsa*, an epic poem of nineteen cantos describing the lives of the Kings of the solar race;

5. *Kumarasambhava*, also an epic poem, of seventeen cantos, dealing with the marriage of Siva and Parvati and the birth of Kumara, the lord of war;

6. *Meghaduta*, a poem of 111 stanzas[1] describing the message of a *Yaksa* to his wife, to be conveyed through a cloud;

7. *Rtu-Samhara*, a descriptive account of the six seasons.

---

[1]Some MSS have a few additional verses.

11

Kalidasa takes up his themes from the traditional lore of the country and transforms them to achieve his object. For example, in the epic story Sakuntala was a calculating, worldly young woman and Dusyanta a selfish lover. The poet wishes to exhibit the sentiment of love from its first awakening in a hermitage girl, to its fullest perfection through the stages of separation, frustration, etc. In his own words, a play must present the diversity of life, and communicate charm and sweetness to men of varied tastes:

Traigunyodbhavam atra loka-caritam nanratam drsyate
natyam bhinna-rucer janasya bahudhapi ekam
samaradhanam.

We do not know any details about Kalidasa's life. Numerous legends have gathered round his name which have no historical value. From his writings it is clear that he lived in an age of polished elegance and leisure, was greatly attached to the arts of song and dance, drawing and painting, was acquainted with the sciences of the day, versed in law and learned in the philosophical systems and ritual practices. He travelled widely in India and seems to have been familiar with the geography of the country from the Himalayas to Kanya Kumari. His graphic description of the Himalayan scenes, of the saffron flower — the plant of which grows in Kashmir, look like those of one who has personal acquaintance.

The master artist suggests, by a few touches, what others fail to express even by elaborate discourses. Kalidasa is famous for his economy of words and naturalness of speech in which sound and sense match. His pen-pictures are graceful and perfect, the royal chariot in full speed,[2] the running deer,[3] Urvasi's bursting into tears,[4] Narad's appearance in the sky

[2]Vikramorvasiya, 1.4.
[3]Abhijnana-Sakuntala, 1.7.
[4]Vikramorvasiya, V.15.

like a moving *kalpa-vrks*.[5] He is master in the use of simile and analogy.

> *Sarasijam anuvidham saivalenapi ramyam*
> *malinam api himansor laksma laksmim tanoti*
> *iyam adhika-manojrid valkalenapi tanvi*
> *kim iva hi madhuranam mandanam nakirtinam.*

'A lotus, though intertwined with moss, is charming. The speck, though dark, heightens the beauty of the moon. This slim one, even with the bark dress, is more lovely. For what is not an embellishment of lovely forms?'[6]

Kalidasa's writings instruct not by direct teaching, but by gentle persuasion as by a loving wife. Mammata says: *kantasammitatayopadesayuje; ramadivat vartitavyam, na ravanadivat.* By an aesthetic presentation of great ideals, the artist leads us to an acceptance of the same. We live vicariously the life of every character that is set before us, and out of it all comes a large measure of understanding of mankind in general. Kalidasa projects his rich and glowing personality on a great cultural tradition and gives utterance to its ideals of salvation, order, love. He expresses the desires, the urges, the hopes, the dreams, the successes and the failures of man in his struggle to make himself at home in the world. India has stood for a whole, integrated life and resisted any fragmentation of it. The poet describes the psychological conflicts that divide the soul and helps us to pull the whole pattern together.

Kalidasa's works preserve for us moments of beauty, incidents of courage, acts of sacrifice and fleeting moods of the human heart. His works will continue to be read for that indefinable illumination about the human predicament which is the work

---

[5]*Ibid.*, Y. 19;
[6]*Abhijnana-Sakuntala*, I.17.

of a great poet. Many of his lines have become almost like proverbs in Sanskrit. *Kumarasambhava* opens with a verse in which the poet speaks as if the Himalayas were the measuring rod spanning the wide land from the east to the western sea.

He suggests that the culture developed in the Himalayan regions may be the 'measuring rod' of the cultures of the world. This culture is essentially spiritual in quality. We are ordinarily imprisoned in the wheel of time, in historicity and so are restricted to the narrow limits of existence. Our aim should be to lift ourselves out of our entanglement, to an awareness of the real, which is behind and beyond all time and history, that which does not become, that which is absolute, non-historical being itself. We cannot think it, enclose it within categories, images and verbal structures.

We know more than we can think and express it in historical forms. The end of man is to become aware by experience of this absolute reality. Compare the words of *Raghuvamsa*: '*brahmabhuyam gatim ajagama.*' The man of enlightenment reaches the supreme timeless life. The performer of good deeds has heaven for his share. We know the Real by the deepest part of our being: *atmanam atmana vetsi.*[7] The Real is the knower and the known: *vedyam ca vedita casi.*[8] Again: *yam aksaram veda-vido vidus tam atmanam atmany avalokayantam.*[9] The Supreme leads a life of contemplation. Though he grants the fruits of others' austerities, he himself performs austerities: *svayam vidhata tapasah phalanam kenapi kamena tapas cacara.*[10]

The Absolute which is the Real beyond all darkness is superior to the division of spirit and matter. It is omniscient, omnipresent and almighty. It manifests itself in the three forms (*trimurti*), Brahma, Vishnu and Siva — the maker, the

---

[7]*Kamarasambhava*, II,10; see *Bhagvadgita*, X.15.
[8]*Kamarasambhava*, II,15; see *Bhagvadgita*, XI.17.
[9]III.50.
[10]I.57.

14

preserver and the destroyer. These gods are of equal rank and a believer may select any form which appeals to him for worship. In daily life, Kalidasa was a follower of the *Saiva system*.[11] The opening invocations of the three dramas *Sakuntala*, *Vikramorvasiya*, *Malavikagnimitra*, show that Kalidasa was a devotee of Siva.

The opening verse of *Raghuvamsa* reads:

vagarthav iva samprktau vagartha-pratipattaye jagatah pitarau vande parvati-paramesvarau.

While in *Malavikagnimitra*, the Lord should set us on the right path, *sammarga*, in *Vikramorvasiya*, he is said to be easily attainable by devotion, *bhakti-yoga-sulabha*, in *Sakuntala*, the Lord in his eight-fold form is seen. Immediate insight into the Divine reality is the aim of religion.

Though Kalidasa worshipped the Divine as Siva, his attitude was not in any way exclusive or narrow-minded. He had the catholic attitude of traditional Hinduism.[12] He treated with great respect the views of others.

Kalidasa has sympathy with all forms of religion and is free from prejudice and fanatacism. Each person can tread the path which appeals to him, for the different forms of Godhead are the manifestations of the One Supreme who is the Formless behind all forms.

tvam eva havyam hota ca bhojyam bhokta ca sasvatah vedtan ca veduta casu dgtata dgtaten ca tat oaran.[13]

---

[11]The cult of Siva worshippers developed around eleventh century.
[12]Yuan Chwang tells us that, at the great festival of *Prayaga*, King Harsa dedicated a stature to the Budha on the first day; to the Sun, the favourite deity of his father, on the second; and to Siva, on the third.
[13]*Kumarasambhava*, II.4, 15.

Raghu, after installing Aja on the throne, retires to the forest, takes to a life of meditation and attains that which is beyond darkness.

tamasah paramapadavyayam purusam yogasamadhina raghuch.[14]

Until the end of religion, the realization of the Supreme, the ascent from the vanity of time is attained, we will have opportunities for making progress towards the goal. In this journey towards the end we will be governed by the law of karma. Kalidasa accepts the theory of rebirth.

ramyani viksya madhurams ca nisamya sabdan
paryutsuki bhavati yat sukhito'pi jantuh
tac cetasa samarati nunam abodhapurvam
bhavasthirani jananantara sauhradani.

Sita, when banished by Rama, says:

When he is born, I'll scorn my queenly station
Gaze on the sun, and live a hell on earth,
That I may know no pain of separation
From you, my husband, in another birth.[15]

This life is one stage in the path to perfection. Even as the present life is the result of our past deeds, we can shape our future by our efforts in this life. The world is under a moral government. The good will ultimately triumph. If we have no tragedies in Kalidasa, it is because he affirms the ultimate reality of concord and decency. Subject to this conviction, he

---

[14]*Raghuvamsa*, VIII, 24.
[15]*Raghuvamsa*. XIV. Ryder's English translation. He refers to the child in her womb.

induces our sympathy for the hard lot of the majority of men and women.

Kalidasa's writings dispose of the misconception that the Hindu mind was attentive to transcendental matters, and neglectful of mundane affairs. Kalidasa's range of experience was wide. He enjoyed life, people, pictures and flowers. He does not separate men from the cosmos and from the forces of religion. He knows the full range of human sorrow and desire, meagre joy and endless hope. He points to a harmony of four main interests of human life, *dharma, artha, kama* and *moksa*, the ethical, the economic, the artistic and the spiritual. The economic including the political and the artistic should be controlled by ethical norms. Ends and means are bound together. Life becomes livable only through valid ties. To cleanse and illuminate those ties was the poet's task.

Kalidasa did not feel called upon to choose between religion and morality on the one side and progress and security on the other. These are not hostile to each other.

History is not a natural but a moral phenomenon. It is not a mere temporal succession. Its essence lies in the spiritual which informs the succession. The historian should penetrate and comprehend that inward moral dynamism. History is the work of man's ethical will, of which liberty and creativity are the expressions.

The kings of the Raghu race were pure from birth, ruled over extensive domains stretching from earth to the ocean, *asamudra ksitisanam.* They amassed riches for charity, spoke measured words for the sake of truth, were eager for victory for the sake of glory, and were householders for the sake of off-spring. They gained knowledge in childhood, enjoyed the pleasures of life in youth, adopted the ascetic life in old age and in the end cast away their bodies by yoga or meditation.

The kings collected revenues for the prosperity of their subjects, *prajanam eva bhutyartham*, even as the sun takes up water to give it back a thousand fold. The rulers must stand up for dharma, justice. The king is the real father of the people, he educates them, protects them and provides for their livelihood, while the actual parents are only the causes of their physical birth.

Every one in Aja's kingdom thought that he was a personal friend of the king.

aham eva mato mahi-pater iti sarvah prakritisvacintayat.

The ascetic tells the king in *Sakuntala*: 'Your weapon is for the protection of the afflicted and not for striking at the innocent', *arta-tranaya vah sastram na prahartum anagasi.* Bharata, the son of Dusyanta and Sakuntala, from whom this country takes its name is called *sarvadamana* — not merely one who conquered every ferocious beast of the forest but has achieved self-control also. Self-control is essential for rulership.[16]

In *Raghuvamsa*, Agnivarna gives himself to dissipation. He has so many mistresses that he cannot always call them by their right names. He develops a wasting disease and as, even in that condition he is unable to resist the pleasures of the senses, he dies.

Kalidasa gives us pictures of the saint and the sage, the hero and the heroine with their nobility. They are the directing minds within a civilization. Nobility and self-control are their distinctive characteristics. Discipline is essential for a decent human life. Kalidasa says: 'Even though produced in a mine, a gem is not worthy of being set in gold, O noble lady, so long as it is uncut.'

---

[16]Kautilya remarks: *bharata iti lokasya bharanat.* He is called Bharata because he supports the world. VII.33.

apyakara samutpanna mani-jatir asamskrta
jata-rupena kalyani na hi samyogam arhati.[17]

Though Kalidasa's works exalt austerity and adore saints and sages, he does not worship the begging bowl.

The laws of dharma are not static and unchanging. The tradition of the past has to be interpreted by one's own insight and awareness. Tradition and individual experience interpenetrate. We are the inheritors of the past but are also trustees of the future. In the last analysis, each one must find the guide for one's conduct in the innermost centre of himself. When Arjuna, in the opening chapter of the *Bhagavadgita*, declines to conform to the demands of society which impose on him as a ksatriya the obligation to fight; when Socrates says, 'Men of Athens, I will obey God rather than you'; they are taking their stand on inward integrity rather than on outward conformity.

In early Vedic literature the unity of all life, animate and inanimate, is indicated and many of the Vedic deities are personifications of striking aspects of nature. The idea of retreat into nature, a mountain top or a forest hermitage, in search of the revelation of the spirit of the universe, has been with us from early times. As human beings we have our roots in nature and participate in its life in many ways. The rhythm of night and day, changes of seasons suggest man's changing moods, variety and capriciousness. Nature had not become mechanical and impersonal for Kalidasa. It had still its enchantment. His characters have a sensitive appreciation of plants and trees, of hills and rivers and a feeling of brotherhood for animals. We see in his writings flowers which bloom, birds which soar and animals which spring. We find a striking description of the love of the cow in *Raghuvamsa*. The *Rtu-*

---

[17]*Malavikagnimitra*, V., 18.

Samhara gives a moving account of the six seasons. It reveals not only Kalidasa's vision of nature's beauty but also an understanding of human moods and desires.

In *Sakuntala* when the curtain rises, Sakuntala and her two friends are seen watering the plants, creepers and trees of Kanva's hermitage, where the stars and colours in the sky, the pretty flowers and the lively animals are vital parts of human experience. Sakuntala does not look upon nurturing the plants as a drudgery, but finds joy in it.

na kevalam tata-niyogah asti mamapi sodarasneha etesu.

— 'not merely because my father has ordered it, I also have fraternal affection for them.'

For Kalidasa rivers, mountains, forests, trees possess a conscious individuality as animals, men and gods.

Sakuntala is a child of nature. When she was abandoned by her *amanusi* mother Menaka, the birds of the sky pick her up and rear her until the sage Kanva takes her under his fostering care. Sakuntala tended the plants, watched them grow and bloom and the occasions when they burst into blossoms and bore flowers and fruits were celebrated as festive days. Like a loving mother Sakuntala reared up her pet animals and plants. No wonder they responded. On the occasions of Sakuntala's wedding, trees sent their gifts, forest deities showered their blessings and cuckoos cooed aloud their joy. The hermitage was filled with grief at the prospect of Sakuntala's departure. The deer drop their mouthfuls, the peacocks stop their dancing and the creepers shed their leafy tears.

When Sita is cast away, the peacocks abruptly stop their dance, the trees shed off flowers, and the female deer throw away the half-chewed *darbha* grass from their mouths:

nrtyam mayurah kusumani
vrkasah darbhanupattan vijahur harinyah
tasyah prapanne sama-dhukha –bhavam
atyantam asid ruditam vane'pi.[18]

Kalidasa takes up an object and creates it for the eye. He had a strong visualizing power. Look at the vivid description of the flight of the antelope which Dusyanta pursues to the hermitage:

grivabhangabhiramam muhur
anupatati syandane baddha-drstih
pascardhena pravistah sara-patana-bhayad
bhuyasa purva-kayam
darbhair ardhavalidhaih sramavivrta
mukhabhramsibhih kirna-vartma
pasyodagraplutatvad viyati bahu-taram
stokam urvyam prayati.

'His glance fixed on the chariot, ever and anon he leaps up peacefully bending his neck; through fear of the arrow's fall he draws ever his hinder part into the front of his body; he strews his path with the grass, half-chewed, which drops from his mouth opened in weariness; so much aloft he bounds that he runs rather in the air than on earth.'

Kalidasa's knowledge of nature was not only accurate but sympathetic. His observation was wedded to imagination. His descriptions of the snows of the Himalayas, of the music of the mighty current of the Ganga, of the different animals, illustrate his human heart and appreciation of natural beauty.

No man can reach his full stature until he realizes the dignity and worth of life that is not human. We must develop sympathy with all forms of life. The world is not made only for man.

---

[18]*Raghuvamsa*, XIV.

21

The love of man and woman attracted Kalidasa and he lavished all his rich imagination in the description of the different kind of love. He does not suffer from any inhibitions. His women have a greater appeal than his men, for they reveal a timeless universal quality, whereas the men are dull and variable. They live on the surface while the women suffer from the depths. The competitiveness and self-assertion of the men may be useful in the office, factory, or battlefield, but do not make for refinement, charm and serenity. The women keep the tradition alive with their love for order and harmony.

When Kalidasa describes feminine beauty, he adopts the conventional account and falls into the danger of sensuous engrossment and sometimes over-elaboration. In *Meghaduta* the *Yaksa* gives a description of his wife to the cloud:

tanvi syama sikhari-dasana pakva-bimbadhrosthi, madhye
ksama, cakita-harini-preksana, nimna- nabhih, sroni-
bharad alasa-gamana, stoka-namra-stanabhyam, ya tatra
syad yuvati-visaye srstir adyeva dhatuh.

'There she lives who is, as it were, the first creation of Brahma amongst women, slim, youthful (or fair in complexion), with pointed teeth, a lower lip red like a ripe *bimba* fruit, thin at the waist, with her eyes like those of a frightened female deer, with a deep navel, slow in gait on account of heavy hips and bending a little low by the weight of her breasts.'

See also the King's description of Malavika in II:

dirghaksam sarad-indu-kanti-vadanam bahu
natavamsayoh samksiptam nibidonnata-stanam urah
parsve pramrste iva madhyah panimitomitam ca
jaghanam pada- varalanguli chando nartayitur yathaiva
manasi slistam tathasya vapuh.

22

'Her face has long eyes and the lustre of the autumnal moon, the arms slope down by the shoulders. Her chest is compact with thick and swelling breasts; her sides are (smooth) as though planed off. Her waist is measurable by the palm of the hand and her hips are broad and the feet have curved toes, and her body is fashioned to suit exactly the fancy of the mind of a dancing master.'

He gives us here a pen-picture of a typical dancing girl which may well make a painter envious.

In the gallery of women Kalidasa presents, we have many interesting types. For many of them the conventional pretences and defences of society did not work. Their conflicts and tensions called for integration. There men felt certain and were secure. They accepted polygamy as the normal rule. But Kalidasa's women had imagination and understanding and so were victims of doubt and indecision. As a rule they were not fickle but trustful, sincere and loving.

Love is deepened by hardships and sufferings borne for the sake of love. It grows a hundred-fold in its intensity by obstacles to its realization, even as the current of a river blocked on its way by uneven rocks (flows with greater force). Even in the absence of fulfilment, the yearning gives all the joy that love means. The pathos of separation finds poignant expression in *Maghaduta*, in *Rati-vilapa* and in *Aja-vilapa*.

Happiness of love in union is found in *Vikramorvasiya*.

In *Malavikagnimitra* the queen is called Dharini because she bears everything. She has dignity and forbearance. When Malavika attracts the notice of the King in a dance scene which the clown has contrived, she rebukes the King in words of harsh satire, that such efficiency would be of advantage if shown in affairs of the state: *yadi rajakaryesv api idrsi upaya-nipunatarya-putrasya tatah sobhanam bhavet*. When her husband's affection shifted to Iravati and then to Malavika, her devotion to him persists. The *parivrajika* Kausiki observes: 'These noble women attached to their lords, serve them even though it be against their own desires.'

By a series of misfortunes, Kausiki is led to the religious life. She comforts and distracts the minds of Dharini. Though a nun, she is an authority on the dance and the cure for snake bite.

Iravati is passionate, impetuous, suspicious, demanding and dictatorial. When she was abandoned in favour of Malavika by the King, she bitterly complains and rebukes the King in harsh words.

Agnimitra's love for Malavika is of the sensual type. The King is fascinated by the beauty and grace of the maid. In *Vikramorvasiya* we have a blend of the human and super human. Urvasi's character is somewhat removed from normal life. She has power to watch her lover unseen and overhear his conversations. She is lacking in maternal affection, for she abandons her child rather than lose her husband. Her love is selfish and her transformation is the direct outcome of a fit of insane jealousy.

Pururavas sings in rapturous terms of love and says that the sovereignty of the world is not as sweet, as blissful, as the lover's labour at the feet of the beloved. The world is dark and desolate to whom love is denied but it is bright and blissful to love triumphant.

In this play we have the development of blossom into fruit, of earth into heaven, of passion based on physical attraction into love based on moral beauty and spiritual understanding. Sakuntala inherits from her mother Menaka, beauty and lightheartedness, and from her father Visvamitra, the famous ascetic, patient and forgiving love. Freedom of sense and austerity of life brought her into being. In her own life the two, freedom and restraint, earth and heaven combine.

In the first Act we find all the impulsiveness of youth. The daughter of the hermitage in the first outburst of passion gave herself away in simple innocence and complete trust to the King. She followed the unsuspecting path of nature as she had not learned to control her feelings and regulate her life by norms.

Dusyanta through forgetfulness, for which the poet does not make him responsible, does not recognize her. He says that he should not look at another's wife, *anirvarnaniyam parakalatram*. Sakuntala suffered the worst that could happen to a devoted wife: she is disowned by her husband and disgraced. Her mind becomes vacant and she stands there lonely, filled with terror, anguish and despair. The poet narrates her endurance of desertion, her fortitude in suffering, her later disciplined life till she is restored to her husband. Love is not a mere affair of the senses; it is kinship of spirit. Both Dusyanta and Sakuntala suffered, were disciplined by sorrow, and obtained the reward of a spiritual harmony. The youthful flush subsides; the gust of passion dies out. Love is won at a higher level and the brief glow of pleasure is turned into a steady life of bliss. Passion is linked with the sanctities of life. Nature and grace blend in harmony.

Kalidasa does not judge the first union of lovers as a moral lapse. They are not sinners but they have to grow through suffering.

Love born of sense attraction should be transformed into love based on austerity and control. While striving to reach heaven, both Parvati and Sakuntala had to skirt the edge of the abyss.

Sex life is not inconsistent with spiritual attainment. Wild life or unrestrained passion is inconsistent with it. Sex life under law and restraint is spiritual in character. One can lead the life of a householder and yet be a hermit in temper. The *Upanisad* says: Enjoy by renunciation, *tyaktena bhunjitha*.

The goal of life is joy, serenity, and not pleasure or happiness. Joy is the fulfilment of one's nature as a human being. We must affirm our being against the whole world, if need be. When Socrates was condemned to death or when Jesus was crucified, they did not take death as defeat but as fulfilment of their ideals. The aim of love is a happy harmony of man and woman. The concept of *ardhanarisvara* brings it out. The wife does not belong to the husband but makes a whole with him.

The wife is the root of all social welfare.

kriyanam khalu dharmyanam satpatnyo mulakaranam

The wife is the *saha-dharma-carini*.

iyan corvasi yavad ayus tava saha-dharma-carini bhavatu.

She is with him in the performance of all his duties. Indumati was to Aja a housewife, a wise counsellor, a good friend, a confidante and a beloved pupil in learning the fine arts.

grhini sacivah sakhi mithah priya-sisya lalite kala-vidhau.

Kalidasa believes that marriage is fulfilled in parenthood. The physical attraction is sublimated through suffering caused by misunderstanding, separation, desertion, cruelty, etc. and attains its fulfilment in the child. The marriage of Siva and Parvati was brought about for the birth of Kumara. This country is named after Bharata, son of Dusyanta and Sakuntala. In *Raghuvamsa*, it is said that the love of Dilipa and Sudaksina increased when it was shared by the love of the son also.

rathanganamnor iva bhava-bandhanam babhuva
yat prema parasparasrayam
vibhaktam apy eka-sutena tat tayoh parasparasyopari
paryaciyata.[19]

---

[19] *Raghuvamsa* III.24.

In *Raghuvamsa*, III. 23, Kalidasa says that Dilipa and Sudaksina rejoiced in the birth of their son even as Uma and Siva were gratified by the birth of Karttikeya, as Saci and Indra by the birth of Jayanta.[20] The marriage of Dusyanta and Sakuntala found its fulfilment in the birth of their son Bharata. The birth of Kumara was the main aim of the marriage of Siva and Parvati. Kalidasa loves children, as is evident from his descriptions of Bharata, Ayus, Raghu and Kumara.

For Kalidasa the path of wisdom lies in the harmonious pursuit of the different aims of life and the development of an integral personality. He impresses on our mind these ideals, by the magic of his poetry, the richness of his imagination, his profound knowledge of human nature and his delicate descriptions of its most tender emotions. We can apply to him the words of Miranda in *The Tempest*.

> *O wonder,*
> *How many goodly creatures are there here!*
> *How beauteous mankind is! O brave new world,*
> *That has such people in't.*

---

[20]*umd Vnsankau sara janmand yatha, yatha jayantena sacipurandarau tatha nrpah sa ca sutena magadhi nanandatus tat samau.*

27

GURU NANAK

— ॐ —

One earth, one family. Goodwill to the whole
of humanity.

Our country's history has witnessed periods of glory
and gloom, triumph and tragedy, victory and defeat.
Whenever we passed through gloomy periods a prophet arose to
call us back to the truth, telling us how we had deviated, how
in our actual life we had disregarded the teachings of the great
seers. Nanak was born in a period of crisis—not political and
social, but moral and spiritual. People were lost in the observance
of trivialities, the celebration of ceremonial piety and the
acceptance of meaningless dogmas, which kept people away from
one another, which separated them, instead of bringing them
together. It was an age of social chaos which was repugnant to
the heart of any right-thinking man. Guru Nanak, therefore
emphasized what may be regarded as the central principles of
any true religion—inward vigilance and outward efficiency. These
are the things on which he laid the greatest stress.

Nanak emphasized on *Omkara*. That is all that he believed
in, but what is *Omkara*? If you try to find out what *Omkara*

means, it is a composite of the three: 'a' 'u' 'ma' (akara, ukara, makara): 'a' stands for the waking state, 'u' stands for the dreaming state, and 'ma' for susupti. All the three taken together, sublimated into one, is pranava or Omkara. Omkara gives you comprehensive reality. It includes the waking, dreaming and dreamless states of human consciousness. There is no other state of human consciousness. All these are, therefore, merged into one Absolute Reality. Guru Nanak did not quarrel about dogmas because Omkara has been said to be invisible, qualityless, unexperienceable — shivam, shantam, advaitam. This is the one fundamental reality, truth is the highest, satnam. God is truth, and there is nothing higher than truth.

Nanak also said that if one wished to understand what this truth was, it was essential for him to enter into the secret chamber of his heart. God is not to be found in the sky above, or in the stars there or in the waters here. He is to be found in the deepest part of man's being. It is that man who is truly religious who is God-intoxicated, who is God-possessed, who has seen into the meaning of existence. It is such people who are regarded as religious in our country, not those who mutter japas, or go to shrines or temples. They may be on the pathway to the Divine, but the man who realizes God is one who sees the Divine in his inmost being.

There is a secret dwelling place in each man's heart, where the Divine is to be felt, is to be touched and experienced. This is what we should do. Prayers, meditations and spiritual exercises are all methods which are devices for helping us to know the deepest in us. This is what the purpose of all true religion is.

This does not mean that we should retire into monasteries or go to mountain tops, lacerate our bodies, torture our minds and give up the world. People who do so are not truly religious. Men who neglect their duties and merely utter the name, krishna, krishna, are the enemies of God; ignorant people who do not know what Reality is. For the sake of humanity,

God himself has taken birth in this world. If He has done that, is it not our duty to express our deepest convictions in our daily life and in our national behaviour?

The time has come when we have to accept Guru Nanak's teachings that names do not matter, that the pathways do not matter. The man who has seen God is truly religious, not those who talk about God and lead atheistic lives. The authentically religious man will never do a thing that is repugnant to his conscience, or that is unholy in any sense of the term.

Guru Nanak told us about *satnam*, the practice of good conduct, the leading of a good life. That is the highest test; *satnam* is great, but greater than that is the practice of love, the practice of compassion. That is what he told us. We talk big and practise little. We all constitute the body of God, and anybody who breaks that body, tears it asunder, is an enemy of God. Are we not doing it every day of our lives? Are we not disintegrating the human being? Are we not breaking this human body into pieces and thus crucifying God Himself? That is what we are doing day after day.

It is, therefore, necessary for us not merely to remind ourselves of the great teachings of Guru Nanak, *satnam* and *sadachara*, but ask ourselves every moment of our lives whether we are really practicing the great teachings that we profess. If we do practice them we will never have these social discriminations, we will never have religious differences. We may start with austerity; austerity will lead to tolerance; tolerance will lead to respect and we will respect what other people hold sacred. Such should be the attitude of a truly religious soul. If you have hatred in your heart, if you have ignorance in your mind, if there is superstition in the dark spaces of your heart, take it from me that you are not a religious man but pretending to be a religious man. A truly religious man will be filled with light, joy and compassion for the whole of humanity.

At a time, when most of us are attached to the things of the world which is becoming increasingly stale and mechanical, becoming intellectualized and secularized, it is good to remember that we have another dimension to our existence and if that is not fulfilled, our life itself is incomplete. Lives of prophets, like Nanak, are an inspiration and a rebuke. An inspiration because they make us feel that there is a side to our existence, a spiritual dimension, which we generally overlook. That is why most of the people in this world today are restless, quarrelling about little things and not realizing that there is the light of lights in each one, *jyotisam jyotih*. It is there in every human being. We overlook it. Because of our overlooking it, we are alienated from our internal being. We live on the surface, but do not get into the depths of our own lives. Most of us lead such outward lives.

Guru Nanak drew our attention at a time when we were forgetting the realities of the world, that there is something pure, changeless, timeless, which persists for all times; he told us about the original rock from which we are hewn, the original spring from which we all derive our existence.

Nanak rebukes us because we have forgotten our own true nature. We live on the surface; we lead superficial lives. Religious life does not mean a life which is withdrawn from the world. Many people think that the lives of saints have a certain grimness and gloom. This is not true. Those who live in God do not take a harsh view of the misfits or the failures of society, and have full compassion for and full understanding of all the ills to which a human being is subject. They understand the vicissitudes through which we pass, the chances and changes; why we trip, why we fall into temptation. So sanctity is not unworldliness; it is a frame of mind, an attitude from which we look at all the things in this world. That is a thing which we all recognize.

The greatest prophets are those who are found feeding the hungry, healing the sick and excusing the sinner. That is the work which they do. We must, therefore, understand that sanctity or holiness is not unworldliness, it is participation in the agony of the world with a proper frame of mind that there is a Supreme Power which can be depended upon and which never fails us.

The other lesson which Nanak taught us is the common ground which subsists between many of our religions. In his time he was faced by antagonism of Hindus and Muslims and he said, 'Why are you quarrelling about forms, about ceremonies, about dogmas, about sacred places, etc. Like this you will find that everyone is worshipping the same Supreme; we are all pilgrims in the same quest. We are all trying to find out where God is, how we can reach him.' That is the lesson which he taught us. There is a common ground between the religions of the world. In his time, Nanak took up Hindus and Muslims and he taught them that the *Quran* and the *Puranas* teach the same thing; whether it is a mosque or a temple, we see the same God. Nanak's rebuke we still deserve because we are still leading superficial lives. We are not truly religious; we are not caught into the depths of our consciousness and do not realize the Supreme who is there. The same Supreme dwells in every human being and if we are quarrelling among ourselves we are crucifying the Lord. The Lord is crucified and His body is torn to pieces. It is necessary for us to understand in this age of mingling of cultures, of religions, etc., that there is a common substratum from which all religions spring. They are the varied expressions of the one and the same Reality. So, there is a spiritual dimension. That sanctity is not withdrawal from the world, that all religions preach the same gospel, and those who are quarrelling about them are not truly religious, these are some of the lessons which Nanak taught us.

It is well known that all great arts centre round religious leaders: music, painting, sculpture, literature, all these centre round and get inspiration from the great religious leaders. Great teachers do teach us these things; they ask us to abolish caste, get rid of untouchability, etc., but it takes a long time for us to practice those teachings. We still suffer from these disabilities. Guru Nanak himself repudiated them and asked us to repudiate them. But we are still practicing them in our lives. We are theoretical believers in Guru Nanak's teachings. Practically, we are giving the lie to the teachings which he gave us. It is, therefore, necessary for us to institute a kind of self-scrutiny and try to wage an inner war, so to say, against false inclinations and appetites from which we all suffer.

We have had with us, from the beginning of history people who told us 'One earth, one family. Goodwill to the whole of humanity,' how many of us have really borne testimony to those great truths in our actual lives? We know today that violence is much more common than it used to be. Why is it that we are unable to adhere to the teachings which these great sages and saints have given to us? Religion is not a thing which you can buy or get from going to a temple, church or gurdwara. It is a thing which you can practise only if you wage incessant war on the baser instincts, which still have so much command over human nature. These are the things which we have to set aside if we wish to be true followers of any great sage or teacher.

The great teachers asked us to become new beings. Have we ever attempted to become new in our character, in our outlook? We are always trying to practise religion with our spinal cord, repeating *mantras* or chanting hymns and thinking that we are religious. But a truly religious man is not made that way. He institutes a different kind of being in his own nature. It is that new being that constituted the greatness of Guru Nanak Dev and it is that thing which we have to bear in mind when we try to adopt his teachings. Caste, untouchability, religious differences — Hindu, Muslim, Sikh, etc., all these things he asked us to set aside and he asked us to remember that we all belong to the one household of God.

SWAMI DAYANAND SARASWATI

—————— ֍ ——————

A social reformer, a crusading zeal,
a powerful intellect.

A mong the makers of modern India, the chief place will be
assigned to Swami Dayanand Saraswati. At a time when
there was spiritual confusion in our country, when many of our
social practices were in the melting pot, when we were overcome
by superstition and obscurantism, this great soul came forward
with staunch devotion to truth and a passion for social equality
and enthusiasm, and worked for the emancipation of our
country, religious, political, social and cultural.

To take the first aspect, the religious one: he was guided by
the rule of reason. We have a number of sayings of his to this
effect: some people worship the waters, the Ganga and so on,
others worship the stars, still others worship images made of
clay and stone; but to the wise man the Supreme dwells in his
own heart, in his own soul. The Supreme is to be found in the
inmost depths of the human being. The culture of our country
accommodated every possible way of approaching the Divine,
and so it gave a place to image worship also.

The supreme place was given to the practice of the presence of God. To get at it, we have to practise dhyana and dharna. But many people are not able to concentrate their minds on the Supreme. Still others are of a nomadic character who cannot be brought even to that stage. Some idea of God must be given to them by any means that one can possibly have, but all the time the one's emphasis must be on the oneness of God. The *Vedas* tell us: of all the Gods, the Supreme original Godhead is one and there cannot be any multiplicity of gods. When we talk of the great souls and *avatars*, we must realize that they are the manifestations of the one Supreme. There is only one Supreme Deity in this world. He may appear in varied forms but do not mistake the shadows for the substance. The Substance is One and Supreme and all our attention must centre round that Reality of which all these are to be regarded as different kinds of manifestation.

This existence of Godhead is not regarded as merely a speculation, or a dogma, or something which you derive from the prophet's words or the sage's words. It is something which you have to acquire by pursuing the rule of reason. Swami Dayanand Saraswati was one who was guided by the supremacy of reason and he made out that the *Vedic* scriptures never asked us to take anything on trust but to examine everything and then come to any kind of conclusion.

We are called upon to find out what the Ultimate Reality is. A father tells his son that from which all things are derived, that by which they are sustained, that into which they are dissolved, that is supposed to be the Supreme Reality. What is *tapas?* Panini tells us *tapas* is reflection, *alochana*. He is looking at the world, trying to find out what this world manifests, what the Supreme Principle which guides this world is, which accounts for the progress that this world has made from a molten mass of fire to the present reality when people like Swami Dayanand have been produced. There is a great *rahasya* found there which accounts for the progress and order of the world. In other words, when we are called upon to practise *tapas*, we are called upon to practise our reason, our reflection, to look at the world, to try judge things by our capacity, to conform to the laws of reason and thought.

In that way he emphasized the rule of reason and pointed out that there is one Supreme God. He also gave freedom of conscience. People may look upon that Supreme as this or that or a third thing. That one Supreme Reality is made out by our heart, by our intelligence and by our will. It is made out in different ways, but we who quarrel about that do not know that the one Reality which is there is the One Supreme without a second. If we really believe in God, if we believe that all human individuals are sparks or fragments of that divine fire, why is it that we have introduced hierarchical distinctions, distinctions of caste and outcaste, and imposed so many disabilities on our women? Here he has to say that if you believe in God, then you must be a believer in the equality of all men and women. You cannot impose restrictions which forbid the study of the *Vedas* or the practice of the *Gayatri japa* to anyone in this world. By virtue of his manhood, of his humanity, everyone is a candidate for spiritual life. And nobody should be denied the privilege of pursuing the greatest fulfilment of his own nature. So not only did he believe in the Supreme but he also enunciated a law of equality of men and women and urged that nobody should be prevented from having access to the spiritual wisdom and the spiritual rituals of our country.

So, he was a social reformer who had a crusading zeal, a powerful intellect and a fire in his heart when he looked at the social injustices. He tried to sweep them away with a drastic hand. This is also what the country requires today. That is why he went from place to place and told the people, 'If you are believers, all believers belong to the one family of God. If you believe in the Supreme, every human individual is a spark of the Supreme. Therefore, you must try to give the best opportunities for the fulfilment of each human individual.'

So, the worship of the One, and the services of man, irrespective of caste, colour and creed, are the two fundamental principles which he formulated. Not only did he formulate them, he went about preaching this gospel, and the Arya Samaj[1] has established many institutions which are today trying to perpetuate these things. Many of these have been incorporated in our social life and practice. Our social legislation after Independence gives equality to men and women; we have tried to remove the disabilities which subjected women to all sorts of atrocities. All these things have become today, a part of our social life.

We should not forget how much we owe to the inspiration of a great man like Swami Dayanand Saraswati; we are adopting the principles which he taught us.

We can strengthen our nation only if we are able to abolish all man-made distinctions, and if we coalesce into a homogeneous community and stand together as one nation. It is this which we are called upon to do now. The teachings which Swami Dayanand Saraswati gave us are of great value today. They are of Supreme importance at a time when we are still bickering and fighting about all sorts of things. Intolerance has been the bane of India. Time and again this country has been subjected to all sorts of slavery. Why? – On account of our internal divisions, on account of our mutual intolerance. If we do not learn from the past, we have to live the past over again. This is the lesson we have to instil into our minds. If we are to learn from the past, the one lesson we need is: forget differences, do not quarrel with one another, believe in the One Supreme and look upon all people as children of that Supreme one.

---

[1] Founded by Swami Dayanad Saraswati in 1875, it became the most powerful movement for Hindu social reform and revival of *Vedic* values in northern India.

RAJA RAMMOHAN ROY

— ❧ —

Inaugurator of modern Indian renaissance.

R aja Rammohan Roy is described as the founder of modern India and the inaugurator of modern Indian renaissance. Renaissance is not merely revival. It takes up ancient wisdom and tries to reconcile it with modern enlightenment; and wherever there is a struggle between the two, it cuts out with a drastic hand whatever is repugnant to reason or to the moral sense.

Raja Rammohan Roy was a believer in human freedom, freedom in every sense of the term. He tried to emancipate the human mind from superstition, from obscurantism, for everything that lowers the dignity of man.

Tapas is reflection on the nature of the universe. Panini tells us, the first word is *lochna*, the second is *alochana*, reflection on the nature of the universe. He winds up by saying that spirit is the Ultimate Reality; not matter or *annam*, not life or *prana*, not mind or *manas*, not *vijñana* or intelligence, but *ananda* or spirit is the Ultimate Reality from which all the others emanate. India, which adopted the *Upanisads* as one of its sacred texts, deviated from their path and lost itself in ceremonial piety and scholastic disputations. It is the mark of a great genius to recall our minds to the fundamental truth.

Moreover, Rammohan Roy studied the classics of Hinduism, Islam and Christianity and found that pure theism was the substance of all religions. On the basis of such a kind of theism it will be possible to integrate not only communities in this country but the whole world. In one of the prayer songs given today, it is made out that there is one Supreme Lord, one Maker of this Universe, described differently. But your heart, by your intelligence, by your will, you give that fact different descriptions, but the Ultimate Substance is one.

There are halting, imperfect descriptions of that One Supreme. If we are able to recognize the reality of the Supreme, we will not fall into controversial paths; because mystery is mystery and our attitude is one of silent adoration. Our words and minds are unable to comprehend the immense mystery of this universe. That is the attitude the human mind must adopt: the human mind is incapable of comprehending adequately the nature of that Supreme.

If we get back to this religion of truth, truth of universal love, then it will be possible for us to forget our petty differences, our trivialities on which we waste our lives; our bigotries and disputations will all lose their force and significance. A truly religious man, if he is authentically religious, will feel that every human being has the dignity, has the spark of Divine. Everyone is a fragment of that impersonal Brahmand, the Universe. You must help everyone to discard all things which prevent his inward life from manifesting itself.

When in this country people were down trodden and our women were subjected to many disabilities, Raja Rammohan Roy raised his voice of protest and said that a country which called itself civilized must accept the basic principle of equality, the equality of all human beings; so long as some people were treated as inferior and others as superior, you were not truly civilized men. This concept of equality was there in our religion in its pristine state. In ancient times women were entitled to every kind of privilege that men had: privileges were given equally to men and women. But centuries passed and this whole concept of equality was dropped and we suffered as a result.

If this country passed through degradation and subjection, it was because we were disloyal to the ideals that we professed. We proclaim high cause of the suffering and subjection to which this country has been put. And if we are to get rid of all these things, we must abolish the disabilities. In practice complete equality should be given to men and women, to the fallen and downtrodden as well as to the privileged.

Raja Rammohan Roy said that he was also for freedom from political subjection, from political tyranny. His contributions to Bengali prose, to the freedom of the Indian press and to love of humanity, and the way in which he appealed to the French Minister and the British legislators about freedom for India, are well known.

There is no question that the great ideals for which Raja Rammohan Roy stood — religion of truth, social equality, unity of mankind — are still our distant goals. We have not realized them. So the message which Raja Rammohan Roy gave us, a message which still has validity, as the ideals for which he lived and died are yet unrealized. They have to be implemented by everyone of us. He was, of course, subjected to persecution, to suffering. That is the lot of all great men. Let me assure you that the world is shaped by the genuine souls who contradict the world most: it is these people who convert the world.

Raja Rammohan Roy stood for equality against caste, for science against superstition, for democracy against dictatorship, for the religion of truth and not a religion of superstition.

ACHARYA JAGDIS BOSE

— ॐ —

A harmonious blend of science, art and religion.

I had the privilege of knowing Jagdis Bose for a number of years when I was a member of the Calcutta University staff. He was the first Indian member of the International Committee of Intellectual Co-operation. Anyone who come to know him was impressed not only by his scientific imagination and inventive skill but also by his pride and patriotism. In him was a harmonious blend of science, art and religion. The Institute, which he founded, is an illustration of his integrated outlook. It is not merely a laboratory but a temple. The working table is an altar. The speech which he made on the occasion of the dedication of the Institute to the nation is a remarkable utterance which makes us thrill with emotions of our past glory and inspires us to greater activities in the future. With a firm conviction that despite all obstacles, truth would prevail, he carried on his impassioned inquiry and research, surmounted the doubt of the learned and the scepticism of the cynics, and established his eminence as a pioneer in the border regions of physics and physiology. His life and work are a triumph of character over circumstance.

India has had a long and continuous history in the development of science. In the seventh chapter of *Chandogya Upanisad* are mentioned the different kinds of knowledge which the learned Narada says that he knows:

rg-vedam, yajur-vedam, sama-vedam, atharvanam, ithihasa-puranam, vedanam vedam, pitrayam, rasim, daivam, nidhim, vakovakyam, ekayunam, deva-vidyam, brahma-vidyam, bhuta-vidyam, ksatra-vidyam, naksatra-vidyam, sarpadevajana-vidyam.

The *Rg-Veda*, the *Yajur-Veda*, the *Sama-Veda*, the *Atharvanam*, the epics and the *Puranas*, grammar which is the *Veda* of the *Vedas*, propitiation of the Fathers, the science of the numbers (mathematics), the science of portents, the science of time, logic, ethics and politics, the science of the gods, the science of sacred knowledge, the science of elemental spirits, the science of serpants and the fine arts.

Indians were greatly interested in ascertaining the laws which govern the different aspects of the universe. They made profound contributions to mathematics, astronomy, grammar, logic, natural sciences and medicine. But for some centuries the scientific genius of India lay dormant.

In the nineteenth century there had been a revival and India again entered into the stream of world science. Dr. Mahendralal Sircar (born: 2 November, 1833) emphasized the importance of scientific knowledge for India's progress. With his passion for science and thirst for knowledge, he founded the Indian Association for the Cultivation of Science, providing facilities for research in all branches of science. Many eminent people, including Professors C.V. Raman and K.S. Krishnan worked in this Association.

Jagdis Bose was a pioneer in research in natural sciences. The great plant physiologist. Professor Heberlandt of Germany after a lecture-demonstration by Jagdis Bose observed: 'It is not an accident that it should have been an Indian investigator who has in such a high measure perfected the methods of the physiology of irritability. In Professor Bose there lives and moves that ancient Indian spirit which has carried to its utmost limits—metaphysical speculation and introspection, wholly withdrawn from the world of sense... that this same spirit should have brought to light in its modern representative, who is our guest today, such an extraordinarily developed faculty for observation and such an ecstasy in scientific experimentation.'

Some of the profound insights of the Indian seers received scientific verification in the researches of Jagdis Bose.

1. The Indian seers look upon the world as a whole and not an aggregate. It is *Puranam*, in the words of the *Upanisad*. It is a universe not a multiverse. Just as in the microcosm of the human system we have *anna, prana, manas, vijñana and ananda,* so also we have them in the macroscosm of the cosmos. *Pinda* and *brahmanda* reflect each other.

2. The world is not a dead expanse but a living universe. The world is called *jagat*, that which moves or is alive. The throb of life is to be found everywhere. The *Isa Upanisad* asks us to know that all this, whatever moves in this moving world is steeped in God.

   isavasyam idam sarvam yat kim ca jagatyam jagat.

3. Nature makes no leaps. There is continuity between the inorganic and the organic, between the living and the animal consciousness. Dharmottara in his *Nyaya-bindutika* notices the contraction of leaves in the night: *svaah ratrau patra-samkocah.*

Udayana mentions phenomena in plants as in the human body: of life, death, sleep, waking, disease, taking medicines, etc.[1]

Jaina and Vaisesika writers, Gunaratna and Samkara-misra mention these characteristics of plants. The sensitiveness to touch of plants like the *mimosa pudica (lajjavati lata)* is noticed. Plants are said to have latent consciousness and are susceptible to pleasure and pain, *antahsamjna bhavanty ete sukha-dukha-samanvitah*. Udyana speaks of the plants as having a dull unmanifested consciousness — *atimandantahsam jnitaya*. Sanskrit poets speak of the *suryamukhi* flowers, which open out in sunlight and shut in its absence. The intuitions of our seers were given empirical verification by Jagdis Bose.

Life activities in the animal and the plant were generally treated as dissimilar. Animals respond to a shock by movement while plants maintain an attitude of passivity even under a succession of blows. Jagdis Bose writes: 'Animal tissues give electric signs of irritation; ordinary plants, according to leading electro-physiologists, show no such signs of excitement. In the animal, again, there is an evolution of wonderful nervous system, by which the organism is put into intimate communication with its different parts and with the environment. In the vegetal organism on the other hand, all authorities are unanimous in declaring that there is no such thing as a nervous impulse even in a plant admitted to be so sensitive as *mimosa pudica*. The two streams of life were said to flow side by side, governed by laws which were altogether different. Jagdis Bose held that the nervous impulse in the plant and the animal was similar. He tried to demonstrate these views by means of delicately contrived instruments.

---

[1] *vrksadayah prati-niyata-bhoktryadhisthitah jivana-marona-svapna-jagarana-roga-bhesaja-prayoga...*

See B.N. Seal: *The Positive Sciences of the Ancient Hindus* (1915), pp. 173-176.

The transition from matter to life, from life to mind may be represented by a slope rather than a staircase. Throughout the cosmos we have continuity and bonds which unite. Jagdis Bose was interested in the latter. While we emphasize the continuity, we should not overlook the creative advance.

A small pebble and a mango seed may be like each other in size, colour, weight, but the difference between them is significant. The pebble may remain the same for a hundred years but the seed has in it the power to become something else. If the conditions are favourable it will gather materials from the soil, from the rain and moisture in the air, from the light and heat of the sun. In time it may become a large tree which may produce in its turn fruits and seeds with the same capacity. The form in which the pebble holds is more rigid than the subtle essence realized in the tree. The tree, unlike the pebble, while persevering towards its end, passes through a cyclic pattern unknown to the pebble. It grows, matures, ages and dies. Unlike the pebble it is subject to disease and is able to reproduce itself.

Science has done many wonderful things but it has not yet explained, much less produced, organic growth and reproduction. The chemical, electrical and electronic process cannot do what a single grain of wheat does, germinate in the spring time. While there is continuity between matter and life there is also a deep difference.

Between life and mind there is continuity. Is the mind always present wherever there is life, say in the organic cell? Is there a boundary between living organism to which mental qualities can be attributed and those to which they cannot?

In his address on the day when he gave his Research Institute to the nation, Jagdis Bose said: 'In the pursuit of my investigations I was unconsciously led into the border region of physics and physiology and was amazed to find boundary lines vanishing. Inorganic matter was found anything but inert; it also was a thrill under the action of multitudinous forces that play on it. A universal reaction seemed to bring together metal, plant and animal under a common law. They all exhibited essentially the same phenomena of fatigue and depression together with possibilities of recovery and of exaltation yet, also that of permanent irresponsiveness which is associated with death. These results were demonstrated by experiments to show the response of matter and the revelations of plant life foreshadowing the wonders of animal life.

Similarly, there is continuity between plant and animal life but life and mind are also different. Impulses from the outer world are transmitted to the brain and constitute its sense data. These are the raw material for perception. We know that consciousness is affected by chemical substances, alcohol, opium, mescalin, anaesthetics and also by concussion. We do not understand what happens in the conscious mind when we have perception, reflection, choice, decision, violation.

Sir Charles Sherrington in his *Man on his Nature* writes: 'The search in that (energy) scheme for a scale of equivalence between energy and mental experience arrives at none. The two, for all I can do, remain refractorily apart. They seem to me disparate; not mutually convertible, untranslatable from one into the other.' In his *Rede Lecture* at Cambridge, he said: 'Strictly we have to regard the relation of mind to brain as still not merely unsolved but still devoid of a basis for its very beginning.' In his last utterance on this subject in a broadcast symposium on 'The Physical Basis of the Mind', his final words were: 'Aristotle, two thousand years ago, was asking how is the mind attached to the body. We are asking that question still.'

True science humbles its votary. It makes him realize how little he knows and how vast is the unknown. No wonder Jagdis Bose, as a seeker for knowledge, felt the mystery underlying the universe. The process of evolution, the stream of creative activity which rolls on, never resting, this perpetual procession of events which we call *samsara* is not self-sufficient

46

or self-maintaining. Look at the succession, a molten mass of fire, the emergence of life, creatures whose forehead recedes, whose teeth protrude, with grunts and groans trying by painful steps to walk on earth, others with articulate speech covered with a sheepskin, carrying a sharp stone and an axe.

Man rubs two stricks together and spark flies, the flame dances. A group of shepherds driving a herd of cattle before them, stop at the edge of a river, glance at the stars and lift their hands in mute appeal for safety and solace. From a nebula, a cloud of gas drifting about in space, the human race has slowly emerged into a Valmiki or a Kalidasa, a Shakespeare or a Goethe, a Newton or an Einstein or Tagore or a Bose. Could it have happened without the inspiration of a higher power working through and directing the process? The *Upanisads* speak of this world as the manifestation of Brahman. Charles Darwin wrote in his *The Descent of Man*: 'That grand sequence of events which our minds refuse to accept as result of blind chance. The understanding revolts at such a conclusion.'

The simple and deep-seated conviction in the human mind that there is a unitary whole which manifests as a manifold, is for the scientist a hypothesis which calls for experimental testimony. For the religious seer it is an act of faith that proves itself in experience. There is no opposition between science and superstition.

Throughout this cosmic process we have continuity and progress. We cannot revive the past but we can build better on the foundations furnished by it. The present shall grow into a nobler future through our efforts. The living spirit of the scientist is a reflection of the Divine mystery. *Tat tvam asi.* Man is made in the image of God and so has to participate in creation. It was Bose's ambition that our people should carry on investigation and research, enrich the world by their results and reach the goal of an enduring brotherhood. Let us work for this goal for the good of mankind and the glory of God.

Jagaddhitaya Krsnaya.

GOPAL KRISHNA GOKHALE

— ತ —

Living without fear or favour.

The attempt of Gokhale was to spiritualize politics. Politics, in those days was not so very complicated as it happens to be today. In those days he felt the need for spiritualization. Today when we have power, when we have authority, when it is possible for us to do so much, how much more is it necessary to spiritualize politics? When we enter politics we enter a region full of passion, prejudice, pride, self-interest, love of power. These are the things which are so much to the top that most of us go about saying, 'There is hoarding, there is corruption, there is dishonesty.' These are the complaints which are made. It is not for me to say how far they are justified or not. All that I say is that the principle of undertaking public work in a spirit of honesty, integrity and dedication is very necessary.

In our country, once upon a time, the question was put: 'What constitutes the principle of a good life? Who is supposed to be a good Man?' The ancient *Upanisad* says: 'Didn't you hear the thunder clap? What did it say? *da da da: datta, damyata, dayadhavam* — charity, self-control, compassion — these are the principles which constitute a good life. It is these principles which we have to take up and adopt in our life, if the level of our political life and public life has to be raised. Gokhale gave us an example of that, whatever subject he undertook, whatever speeches he made; we used to listen in our student days to those speeches, read about them, as there was no radio, we had to read them in the newspapers. We were all struck by his intense patriotism, when he rebutted the charge that universities were seats of sedition and that educational institutions were breeding people in a kind of inflammatory atmosphere.

When we listened to all those things we were greatly thrilled. But what constitutes his greatness? His greatness consisted in making a thorough preparation of any subject that he undertook, a careful study of facts, and then scrupulous judgement on the facts, justified condemnation or approval. Those who undertake public life today, will have to regard themselves as wholetime workers, make a thorough study of the political problems of the country and then come to judgements which are reasonable and reasoned. That is what they should do. But are they doing it?

From Gokhale we inherited a tradition — a tradition which calls upon us not to sacrifice the individual at the altar of the State or any kind of system. But to protect the individual, save his rights, regard him as someone sacred. That gives us the justification for the attitude which we are adopting. It is necessary, therefore, that we should regard the individual as the end and not the State as the end. We should regard his rights as inviolable. It may be necessary to sacrifice our life, but we should do so with all respect to ourselves and with integrity.

In spite of all the objectives which we have professed, there are social disparities in our society, high and low, rich

49

and poor, high caste men and outcastes, untouchables, etc. Have we come to the end of the task? Is not our present position a challenge to us? Are we not called upon to adopt the right kind of attitude in the handling of these problems?

Why did Gandhi feel attracted to Gokhale? For the simple reason that Gokhale would not surrender truth, would not sacrifice it for the sake of any political idea or ideology. He would stand firm so far as his attitude was concerned and give out his opinion without fear or favour, without any kind of ill-will or malice toward anybody. Even the opponents whom he had to deal with had respect for him. Whether they liked him or not, whether they liked his opinions or not, they had considerable respect for the integrity of the individual and for the careful study which he always made of the facts; and for the brilliant Budget speeches that he made in the Central Assembly in those days, he will be remembered for many long years to come.

Are we, or are we not, to follow his example? If we see the way in which our Assemblies and Parliament are functioning now, we think that there is great need of spiritualization of politics today; everyone who enters the Assembly or Parliament should regard himself as a servant of humanity, as a servant of India and should not do anything which is likely to impair the prestige of or respect for the State.

In accordance with the traditions of our country Gokhale emphasized the need for renunciation in public life. *Servam vastu bhayānvitam bhuvi nrinām vairāgyam evābhavam.* While everything in this world is fraught with fear for men, renunciation alone gives fearlessness. When the comforts of the world were in Gokhale's reach and could have been his, he left them and gave his great talents to the service of the country. Renunciation is the principle of a good life. Men are great not by what they acquire but by what they renounce.

Those who engage in public work should not look upon it as a career with glittering prizes.

When twenty years old, Gokhale joined the Deccan Education Society to serve it for twenty years on a small allowance of Rs. 75 per month. In 1905 he founded the Servants of India Society and set up a body of dedicated persons. The members participated in varied activties—education, journalism, politics, tribal welfare, etc. guided by Gokhale's dictum that: 'Public life must be spiritualized. Love of country must so fill the heart that all else shall appear as of little importance by its side. A fervent patriotism which rejoices at every opportunity of sacrifice for the Motherland, a dauntless heart which refuses to be turned back from its object by difficulty or danger, a deep faith in the purpose of Providence which nothing can shake — equipped with these, the worker must start on his mission and reverently seek the joy of spending ourselves in the service of the country.' No wonder that Gandhi claimed Gokhale as his political guru.

Gokhale insisted not only on intellectual efficiency but also moral responsibility for the members of the Society. Today in the selection of candidates for legislatures or other public bodies we do not seem to insist on the purity of the means. We seem to be possessed by considerations of caste or community and not those of character or capacity. The disorder in the country is traceable to this factor also.

Gokhale enrolled in his Society members like G.K. Deodhar, a valiant fighter for social reforms; N.M. Joshi, who influenced the Trade Union Movement; Srinivasa Sastri, who served in varied capacities; he had with as the first member H.N. Kunzru, a man of integrity and uprightness, an example to others. Gandhi and Nehru seriously thought of joining the Society. If any one leads a dedicated life, if he is devoted to truth, if he avoids intrigues in public life, he is a religious man though he may call himself an agnostic.

When Gokhale visited South Africa in 1912, a well-known statesmen-senator said to him, 'Sir, when men like you visit our country, they purify the atmosphere.'

Those trained by Dadabhai Naoroji, Pherozeshah Mehta and Ranade believed in moderation. Life is one whole. Political progress and social reform cannot be separated. Life cannot be compartmentalized. Gokhale sympathized with the poor and the oppressed. In his evidence before the Welby Commission he gave expression to the growing poverty of the country under British rule.

Gokhale had deep faith in democratic principles, civil liberties, a free press, free association, hatred of racial discrimination of any type, decent standards of living for all. He was an ardent advocate of free and compulsory education.

Political or religious reformers are critical of the conditions round them but if they are liberal they would not have the sensation of hate. They would be free from the feeling of hate while they are eager to improve the existent conditions.

Gokhale's liberalism would not forbid him from adopting Gandhi's passive resistance. In a speech on Indians in Transvaal at a public meeting in Bombay in 1909, Gokhale said: 'Passive Resistance to an unjust law or an apprehensive measure is a refusal to acquiesce to that law or measure and a readiness to suffer the penalty instead, which may be prescribed as an alternative. If we strongly and clearly and conscientiously feel the grave injustice of a law, and there is no other way to obtain redress, I think refusal to acquiesce in it, taking the consequence of such refusal, is the only course left to those who place conscience and self-respect above their material or immediate interests.'

The problems facing India in Gokhale's time were formidable. Though he served all sides of our life in a brilliant and wholehearted manner he was conscious of the long distance we have to traverse before we reach the goal. He had faith in the destiny of his country: 'It will, no doubt, be given to our countrymen of the future generations, to serve India by their successes; we of the present generation must be content to serve her by our failures. For hard though it be, out of those failures, the strength will come, which in the end will accomplish great tasks.'

Sarojini Naidu described Gokhale as 'the greatest saint and soldier of our national righteousness, whose life was a sacrament and whose death was a sacrifice in the cause of Indian unity.' Ministers of good things are like torches, a light to others and a destruction to themselves.

The lesson which we have to learn from Gokhale's life is that we are to improve ourselves, have an element of reverence for Ranade, reverence for Dadabhai Naoroji, Pherozeshah Mehta, reverence for Gandhiji. That element of reverence is fast disappearing from our life. It is this that we should re-emphasize. We should be grateful to people who put us on the right track. And next to reverence was his principle of renunciation. Things come and go. Prestige disappears in a few days. Today one is a great men, tomorrow he is brought down. That is how it is, *Vibhava Saiva Sasvatah*. All this pomp and glory are not eternal. Reverence for life and renunciation, if you adopt these two principles you will serve Gokhale and his memeory well.

Our country has been famous for its great sages and saints. History is not a battle of kings, is not merely an account of what happened between dynasties. History is a march of social changes, new economic structures, new movements which happen in this world. They are the things which matter in the life-time of a nation. So far as our nation is concerned, the things that happened in Gokhale's time, the work that was done, the political movements, social movements, religious reforms, all these things which happened, stand together. They are not to be kept apart. They are to be regarded as parts of one whole. It is essential, so far as our country is concerned, that we should stick to the framework of our religions, our widest landmarks, so to say, which will always be there, because the scientists may touch the periphery but nobody touches the centre.

If we concentrate on the centre of our being, we will realize that there is an aspect, a universal nature, a universal right, which gives utterance to all the other things we have. In other words, our intellect, our mind, our growth, all these things are the expressions of that universal centre which each one has. Because we are trying to forget that centre, many of us are getting alienated from ourselves and are suffering from neuroses and disturbances.

Let us develop reverence, let us develop respect, for the central principle of our being and let us have renunciation. We will go forward.

What touches human hearts is the power of faith. It comes only to those who have suffered greatly. Though Gokhale knew Dadabhai Naoroji, Gandhi, Tilak, his heart was given to Mahadev Govind Ranade, who gave him the ideals which Gokhale illustrated in his life. In the prospectus of the Deccan Sabha, Ranade said:

Liberalism and moderation will be the watch-words of our Association. The spirit of liberalism implies a freedom from race and creed prejudices and, a steady devotion to all that seeks to do justice between man and man, giving to the rulers the loyalty that is due to the law that they are bound to administer, but securing at the same time to the people the equality which is their right under the law. Moderation implies the conditions of never vainly aspiring after the impossible or after too remote ideals but striving each day to take the next step in the order of natural growth by doing the work that lies nearest to our hands in a spirit of compromise and fairness.

Gokhale easily identified himself with the condition of his people and consistently tried to raise it. Public work, Gokhale felt, should have intellectual and moral foundations. Leadership, to be effective, should have moral authority. His attempt was to spiritualize politics. Anyone who leads a dedicated life, who is devoted to truth, and who avoids intrigue and factionalism in public life, he is a religious man though he may call himself a pagan or agnostic. Whatever work Gokhale undertook, he threw himself into it, heart and soul. As a Professor in Fergusson College or as a member of the Central Legislative Council, or as a member of the Bombay University or the Poona Municipality, thoroughness marked his work. Gandhi came to know Gokhale well and felt that he was the one whom he could accept as his guru. Gandhi said of Gokhale:

He seemed to me, all I wanted as a political worker — pure as a crystal, gentle as a lamb, brave as a lion, and chivalrous to a fault. It does not matter to me that he may not have been any of these things. It was enough for me that I could discover no fault in him to cavil at. He was, and remains for me, the most perfect man in the political field.

BALGANGADHAR TILAK

— ॐ —

Unafraid and forthright, one who laid the foundation
of Indian nationalism.

When I was a student in the early years of this century,
the name of Tilak meant for the youth of the country
— burning patriotism, rare courage, indomitable will and
dedication to the freedom of India.

In the second decade, I happened to write an article in
July 1911, on *The Ethics of the Bhagavadgita and Kant* which
attracted the attention of Tilak who was then in Mandalay
prison (now in Myanmar). The late Shri N.C. Kelkar wrote
to me for that article which he sent to Tilak. In due course
the article was returned to me with Tilak's marginal notes.
I found to my great joy that Tilak mentioned my name in
his preface to that monumental work, *Gita Rahasya*, as one
who supported an activistic interpretation of the *Bhagavadgita*.
Even the liberated are called upon to work for world
solidarity, *lokasamgraha*, for the good of the world, the glory
of God. *Jagad-hitaya-krsnaya*. The *Gita* is a *yogasastra*. Yoga
is *karmasu kausalam*, skill in action. *Samatvam yoga ucyate*.

Equanimity is yoga. *Krsna* is *yogesvara*. He is the Lord of action.

viveki sarvada muktah kurvato nasti kartrta
alepa-vadam asritya sri-krsna janakau yatha.

The spiritual and social sides go together. Tilak's life was a demonstration of this great ideal of Karma Yoga. The saints of Maharashtra — Jnaneshwar, Eknath, Tukaram, Ramdas, proclaim that disinterested service of man is the worship of God.

In ordinary circumstances Tilak would have lived a scholar's life, and made outstanding contributions to Oriental Studies and Mathematics. But as a member of a subject nation he had no alternative except to take part in politics. When once he was asked: 'What portfolio will you take up when we obtain Swaraj? Will you be Prime Minister or Foreign Minister?' his answer showed where his heart lay. 'Under Swaraj, I will become a Professor of Mathematics and retire form political life. I detest politics. I still wish to write a book on Differential Calculus. The country is in a very bad way and so I am compelled to take part in politics'; and what a part! He was not in sympathy with the methods of those who were then called Moderates. He transformed the political movement limited to the upper classes into a national one. By the use of popular festivals and through the medium of his well-known Marathi paper *Kesari*[1] he spread the message of 'Swaraj as our birthright' to the common people. He advocated a vigorous programme of national education, Swadeshi, boycott, passive resistance including the non-payment of taxes. His plan included prohibition and removal of untouchability. In his hands the political movement became

---

[1]Marathi newspaper founded by Balgangadhar Tilak.

a revolutionary one, but revolution is not to be confused with barricades and bloodshed. He repudiated methods of violence. When political and social conflicts were tense, he affirmed that in such matters 'fanaticism is suicidal'.[2] When violence was in the air, Tilak wrote in *Kesari* as long ago as 1904: 'The British administration does not depend upon any one person at any time. Therefore, nobody can get Swaraj by killing an officer and even if one could get it, murder is absolutely reprehensible. It is cowardice to incite anyone to commit murder. But if necessary, we should suffer for our convictions.'

When he was condemned to a six-year sentence, he said: 'There are higher powers than this tribunal that rules the destinies of beings and it may be the will of Providence that the cause I represent will prosper more by suffering than by my remaining free.' No wonder Gandhiji, when he was condemned to a similar sentence, and the judge observed: 'You will not consider it unreasonable, I think, that you should be classed with Mr. Tilak,' said, 'Since you have done me the honour of recalling the trial of Lokamanya Balgangadhar Tilak, I just want to say that I consider it to be the proudest privilege and honour to be associated with his name.'

Tilak repeatedly said: 'Swaraj is the foundation and not the height of our future prosperity. We have to build a new nation, develop a new character, live the principles which we advocate, faith in spiritual values, love of country and tolerance for views from which we differ.' The perspective of history will record that in Tilak we had an Indian, true and great, proud of his country's past and confident about its future, a patriot unafraid and forthright, one who laid the foundations of Indian nationalism and revolutionary struggle through non-violent political action.

---

[2] *Kesari*, 7.6.1892

MOTILAL NEHRU

— ॐ —

Faith in the spirit of man to mould history.

The services which Shri Motilal Nehru rendered to this country's struggle, progress and prosperity are many, varied and outstanding. But I am concerned with the special contribution which he made to the development of parliamentary institutions. He happened to be the Chairman of All-Parties Committee which was asked to draft a Constitution for our country in 1928. That Constitution included, among other features, the declaration of rights and the setting up of a judiciary with a Supreme Court at its apex. Parliamentary democracy was the primary thing.

Faith in the infallibility of any individual or nation is at the root of all conflicts in this world. It breeds fanaticism, sets up dictatorships, brings about fascism of the mind which has often drenched this earth with blood and tears. It is, therefore, essential for us to avoid that kind of dogmatic attitude. A democratic attitude requires appreciation that the other man may possibly be right and that we ourselves may be in the wrong, an attitude of modesty, humility, good manners and charity—these are the essential qualities of a democratic frame of mind. If we wish to work democratic institutions successfully and satisfactorily opinionatedness; dogmatism, an idea that we alone have the monopoly of truth and that others are revelling in the dark, are things which we should avoid.

In international relations, this requires us to settle all outstanding differences by persuasion, negotiation and mediation. A climate of international sobriety has to be engendered if the world is to be made a happy home for the different nations of the world. In both these respects, Shri Motilal Nehru set us a great example. He was Leader of the Opposition in the Central Legislative Assembly for six years. The Opposition had a number of members belonging to different persuasions. He brought them all together, organized them into a single team and he made the then Assembly reject four successive budgets. He moved a Resolution on self-government for India which was passed by 76 votes to 48, the opponents being official and other nominees.

The great point about his achievement was that he had no malice in his heart, no bitterness, and that he commanded the confidence and affection of his followers and the respect and admiration of his opponents. The whole thing took place in a quiet and dignified way. There was no greater problem in our country then than the achievement of self-government. In the Central Assembly was waged a battle between Indian nationalism and foreign domination and he prepared the ground for the achievement of freedom. He gave us a magnificent example of dignified, disciplined behaviour which we should remember whenever we enter the precincts of Parliament.

He not only taught us about Parliamentary democracy, but he knew that no freedom was worth its name unless it brought about national cohesion. He was aware of the way in which religion was confused with bigotry, a kind of superiority-complex that one had the monopoly of all truth and that others were groping in the dark; he was aware that it was one's duty to get rid of that feeling. He knew the dangers of such kind of attitude. He protested against the mixing of religion with politics and he insisted that all our brethren must be considered as citizens of our country and that they should not be looked down upon on the basis of caste. He asked us to build up a coherent society.

There is another thing which I should like to remind you all about: he served on the Skeen Committee, a committee which was entrusted with the setting up of National Defence Colleges. We are all working for a time when armies, etc., would not be necessary. But that time is still far away. But until that time comes, it is essential for us to keep our armies intact, to see that they are modern and well-equipped, so that no people can take liberties with us. It is therefore incumbent on us to remember what he did on the Skeen Committee.

The purposes of our Constitution or society are based on the principles which he framed. The purposes are there but we have to achieve them by our own drive, energy, enterprise, organization and by the stigma of the love of power and the love of self-interest, and by development of rectitude. These are essential for the carrying out of the aims which we have set for ourselves.

Motilal Nehru's life blended with the life of the country. After independence we have been trying to translate his ideals into offective reality. It will take us a long time before we can say that democracy is functioning here irrespective of caste, community, race and religion. But every one of us must look upon himself as a dedicated servant of that noble cause, which will lift us out of our own pusillanimity and make us worthy of a great cause, a modern civilized society.

I met Motilal Nehru for the first time when he came to Calcutta for presiding over the Congress session in 1928. In the same year he produced what is called the Nehru Report, our first effort at Constitution-making. I saw him also when he was leading the Swaraj Party[1] in the Central Assembly here. I met him again a few weeks before his death when he was undergoing treatment in Calcutta. His thoughts in those last days were about Swaraj for which he worked with such devotion and fervour. On his death-bed at Allahabad, Motilal Nehru was waiting for Gandhiji. When he came, Gandhiji said, 'We shall surely win Swaraj, if you survive this crisis.' Motilal Nehru said, 'I am going soon, Mahatmaji, and I shall not be here to see Swaraj. But I know you have won it and will soon have it.' Our greatest sorrow is that he did not live to see that day.

The name of Motilal Nehru will be permanently inscribed in the annals of our history not only for his individual contribution, but for his greatest and noblest gifts to this nation and the world, Jawaharlal Nehru. Motilal's whole family was inspired by his example and with the influence of Gandhiji, became a part of the national movement.

Motilal Nehru had an enfranchised mind, free from all prejudices, hospitable to all good influences, Hindu, Muslim and British.

His appearance reminded us of the ancient Roman consuls. He had a regal presence, a lordly manner and moved through the world on a high plane and dominated every gathering. He had not the taint of commonness but had a distinction in his manner.

He was a great lawyer, a great patriot, a great man, who was incapable of anything mean or dishonourable. His personal and powerful character won him esteem from both Indians and the British. In every sense of the word, Motilal Nehru was a magnanimous man.

---

[1]*Swaraj Party* was formed by C.R.Das as a result of his differences with Gandhiji on non-co-operation movement.

It is possible to give a long list of the attributes and achievements of the late Pandit Motilal Nehru, his qualities of leadership and warm humanity, his patience and persistence, his determination and energy, his courage and force. All these have stamped his mark indelibly on the public life of our country. However, I shall confine myself to the political and social activities of Motilal Nehru.

The credit for Motilal's entry into politics goes to Gandhiji and Jawaharlal, apart from the forces of history. 'He is no brave man whose spirit does not rise when things are at their worst.' Though accustomed to a very comfortable life and regarded as a great admirer of Western style and manners, he subjected himself to the discipline which Gandhiji imposed on his followers. Gandhiji made spinning the basis of his constructive programme. Spinning and wearing of khaddar had become obligatory for political workers; khaddar became the bond of sympathy between the political workers and the millions of Indians. He cast aside his foreign dress and put on khaddar in Indian style and looked even more impressive and attractive in his new style. He joined the Civil Disobedience Movement in 1930[2] and suffered imprisonment.

In his political activities, two things stand out prominently. He was a great organizer, a great parliamentarian, and as the leader of the Swaraj Party in the Central Assembly, he set standards which we are striving to follow. From the visitors' gallery, I saw him on occasions at work in the Central Assembly as the Leader of the Opposition. Most distinguished in appearance as in intellect, he led the Opposition with great astuteness, legal acumen and parliamentary skill. He organized

---

[2]A mass no-violent movement under the leadership of Mahatma Gandhi, denying the legitimacy of the British rule and refusing to pay taxes.

opposition to the Simon Commission in 1928.[3] He presided over the All-Parties Conference and drew up a Constitution for the country. The same year, 1928, he was the President of the Calcutta session of the Indian National Congress. It was a great joy for him to see Jawaharlal take over from him as Congress President. He quoted a Persian couplet which said, 'What the father has not been able to achieve, the son will.' He said that it would be ' the head of Gandhiji and the voice of Jawaharlal.' In December 1929, the Lahore Congress Session under the Presidentship of Jawaharlal Nehru passed a resolution about the independence of India. It was passed by an overwhelming majority exactly at midnight and with it the new year and the new era commenced.

Apart from his parliamentary work, Motilal Nehru laid the greatest stress on communal harmony and unity. It was not a mere tactical move on his part, but a deep-felt conviction, a part of his very being. When the country was torn by communal strife and when bitterness and violence were rampant, Gandhiji undertook a fast. Motilal presided over the Unity Conference and on September 26, 1924, the Conference resolved that 'the utmost freedom of conscience and religion was essential, and condemned any desecration of places of worship, to whatever faith they may belong, and any persecution or punishment of any person for adopting or reverting to any faith; and it further condemned any attempts by compulsion to convert people to one's faith or to secure or enforce one's own religious observance at the cost of the rights of others.' This faith in communal harmony and religious fellowship is needed even today. Though we suffered in the past for our religious bigotry and communal

---

[3]A statutory commission led by Sir John Simon, to investigate the working of Montagu-Chelmsford Reforms, which were a 'half-way house' to responsible government in which all important subjects were reserved for the Governor-General's discretion, while unimportant subjects were transferred to local government.

dissensions, we have not yet learnt the needed lesson. The canker of communalism is deep-seated in our body politic. We should do our utmost to root it out and cleanse our natures.

Motilal was a radical reformer not out of any false sentiment but for a very cool reason. Communal passions are inconsistent with the true spirit of religion or the traditions of our country.

Jawaharlal Nehru told Gandhiji that in the last moments of his life, Motilal repeated the *Gayatri Mantra* though he had never uttered it for nearly 40 years. According to it, God is no longer an irate father or a stern judge but the Light of Lights, *Jyotisam Jyotih*, Spirit of Light shining in the future, a Light towards which we all endeavour to advance with the faltering steps owing to our own unworthiness. Deep down he had faith in Indian culture and its freedom of spirit, its capacity for healing the ills of men and nations. Motilal Nehru's life was marked by an essential fidelity to civilization, by respect for human dignity and craving for human fellowship.

Indian culture has survived for nearly sixty centuries. Though it passed through many ups and downs, it has come down to us with its unfathomable depths and great capacity for devotion and service. What constitutes the national spirit or genius springs from deep and ancient, all the time diverting and altering their course, now in flood but on occasions parched and dry. These are the imponderables· that bring history home to our consciousness and make facts look stranger than fiction. We have suffered defeat on many occasions. These misfortunes have not broken our spirit. After every blow, India found herself again, and made advances in spite of pain and sorrow. Today, we are in one of the creative epochs of our history. We are trying our best to remould our heritage with insight into the profundities and with awareness of the demands of our age. Motilal was not a victim of the blind fatality of history in a violent age. He had faith in the spirit of man to mould history.

LALA LAJPAT RAI

— ☙ —

'Men like Lajpat Rai cannot die as long as sun shines
in the Indian sky.'
— *Mahatma Gandhi*

Lala Lajpat Rai, is generally known as the Lion of the
Punjab. When we were students, we were deeply moved
by the arrests and deportations of Lala Lajpat Rai and Sardar
Ajit Singh. I had the honour of meeting Lala Lajpat Rai at
Pandit Madan Mohan Malaviya's house at Banaras in the
twenties, a few years before his death. I later saw him at work
in the Central Assembly as a member of the Swaraj Party
under Pandit Motilal Nehru's leadership.

Lajpat Rai started his life as a lawyer at Hissar and then
moved to Lahore where he built up considerable prestige and
a lucrative practice at the Bar. He was impressed by the
inadequacy of many of the pernicious social practices and
forms which had crept into the Hindu faith and wished to
free society from these social evils. He recognized that until
we had won political freedom it would not be easy to rid our
society of these grave disabilities from which many of its
members, especially the women, had suffered. So, Lala Lajpat

Rai became an ardent fighter for political freedom as well as a courageous crusader against caste, untouchability and the subjection of women.

He looked upon education as the main instrument for achieving social and national progress. On the death of Swami Dayanand Saraswati, the D.A.V. College was established at Lahore and it was used by Lala Lajpat Rai as a powerful instrument of national education and progress.

In 1920 he returned from the United States and immediately his grateful countrymen elected him as the President of the special session of the Indian National Congress at Calcutta. He joined the Swaraj Party founded by Motilal Nehru, C.R. Das and others, and was elected to the Central Assembly. Under his leadership the Central Assembly passed a resolution advocating the boycott of the Simon Commission. He followed the resolution by his personal example and, when the Simon Commission actually arrived in Lahore in 1928, he led a procession expressing India's resentment against the Commission. The police dispersed the crowd with lathi-charges and Lajpat Rai received serious injuries from which he never recovered. He passed away on the November 17, 1928.

Many members of the Swaraj Party were not quite sympathetic to Gandhiji's methods of civil disobedience and non-violent non-cooperation for gaining political freedom. In the first issue of *The People,* Lajpat Rai's differences with Gandhiji's programme were expressed clearly. He wrote: 'Melodrama and an excessive sentimentality have no place in politics. For some time we have been busy making experiments with schemes which could not possibly be carried out without an immediate radical change in human nature. Politics deals primarily and essentially with the facts of a nation's life and the possibilities of its progress in the light of these. Human nature cannot be changed in months and years. You may require decades, even centuries, for that. Prophets and dreamers and visionaries are the salt of the earth. The world would be much poorer without them. But a campaign of political emancipation of a nation under foreign rule imposed and maintained at the point of the bayonet cannot be based on an attempt to change human nature quickly. Such attempts are bound to fail and end in disastrous action.' Lajpat Rai did not live to see the fruition of Gandhiji's attempt to win freedom by peaceful methods.

At a time like the present, when in different parts of the world there are wars and the piling up of nuclear armaments, it is wise to remember that there is no other way for the safety of the world than that taught by Gandhiji. We may suffer but we should not inflict suffering on others. International conflicts can be resolved by peaceful methods if we have the will and the patience and the forbearance necessary for them. It is true that moments may come when human nature feels itself justified in meeting one wrong with another. But our recent history is a living protest against any such precipitate action.

Even though Lala Lajpat Rai did everything in his power to fight discrimination among the people, we still discriminate in the name of caste or community, race or religion. These hurt the pride of those who are discriminated against and Lajpat Rai was greatly disturbed by these activities. He was a firm believer in social equality. If there is any lesson which we have to learn from the life and work of Lajpat Rai, it is that political stability can be based only on social equality. We have to carry out the fight against inequalities imposed on us by force of custom or the authority of the past. Lajpat Rai's burning patriotism, his capacity to take risks and submit to suffering, his exile in Britain and America, his deportation and martyrdom, showed the stuff of which he was made. Writing on his death, Mahatma Gandhi said: 'Men like Lajpat Rai cannot die as long as the sun shines in the Indian sky.'

RABINDRANATH TAGORE

— ॐ —

A world citizen: a *viswa-manava*.

R abindranath Tagore raised the stature of our country in
the eyes of the world. He was a versatile genius, a literary
artist, an educator, a composer, a singer, an actor. Nature was
liberal to him in her gifts and fortune in her favours. Dr. Roy
said that his outlook was based not on knowledge but vision.
Rabindranath does not give us a system of philosophy but
gives us flashes of light which illumine our minds and warm
our hearts. His work does not so much convey a message as
embody a vision. To lift man out of the stale air of common
life, to regions where the eternal verities are seen undimmed
by self or sophistry and man's ordinary existence becomes a
life, a passion, a power, this was Rabindranath's life-mission.

A man of genius is said to be compounded of the qualities
of a man, woman, and a child, of vigour, of intellect, intensity
of feeling and perpetual wonder of a child. These are not
exclusive traits. There are women with great vigour of intellect
as we know to our cost. All of us have in some degree the
sense of curiosity, of wonder.

Born in a reformed Hindu family, Rabindranath pleaded not only for concord with the past, but also for freedom from the past. All healthy growth needs continuity and change. We are not free unless our minds are liberated from dead forms, tyrannical restrictions and crippling social habits. Every fresh movement of spirit means the casting off of the old body, of the garments. Rabindranath felt that the Indian people were much too self-centred and lazy in their minds to get over prejudices, stupid and violent.

He condemned the corruption of many of our social practices. While a stagnant pool breeds malaria and mosquitoes, a living current cleanses its waters as it hurries along. Perpetual renewal and rededication to self-development are the essence of life.

Rabindranath's great works sprang from intensity of vision and feeling. In his literary works he spoke of that province of human life, vast and boundless, with its affections and sympathies, loves and friendships, joys and sorrows of which mere intellect does not speak. He sang of beauty and heroism, nobility and charm, resignation and despair, the fervour of revolt and the shame of defeat. When we read this great poet, we see the world with rechristened eyes. His songs are sung not only in Bengal but all over the country.

He has given innocent joy to many children by his stories like *Kabuliwalah*. He gathered fragments of moonlight and distilled them into words as in his *Crescent Moon*.

He did not live in an ivory tower. He led a procession in 1905 through the streets of Calcutta singing his song 'Are you so mighty as to cut asunder the bond forged by Providence?' Millions of voices have sung the National Anthem: *Jana Gana Mana*, calling upon us to nourish the unity of our country and be devoted to it.

Genius is distant vision: *dura drsti*; it is anticipating experience. Rabindranath felt the destiny of the world as a fellowship of people. His Visva-Bharati was a world university, a preparation for the distant goal where the world makes a home in a single nest: *yatra visvam bhavati ekanidam*. All races and nations belong to the one world. A commonwealth of mind and spirit is a prelude to a political commonwealth. Tagore was a world citizen: a *visva-manava*.

He was not only a poet and a playwright but a novelist and a story teller, a composer and an actor, a serious thinker and a social reformer, an educator, a nationalist and an internationalist. As if these activities were not enough, he turned to painting towards the end of his life. He rejected traditional canons and experimented with new forms and colour compositions. His paintings and sketches — more than 1,500 of them are preserved — take us to the realm of the fantastic and the unreal. We honour him not only for this many-sided genius but also for the guidance of his life and work in this troubled world.

He built a monument for himself not merely as a record of achievements but also as a lesson to posterity. The world claims him as its own because of what he became, and what millions of human beings hunger to become. He attained that perfect co-ordination of being that belongs to genius, that serenity of mind sought by many and achieved by few.

The urgent need of the human race is to move a step forward in its evolution. Rabindranath's mission was one of reconciliation between East and West in a spirit of understanding and mutual enlightenment. 'All humanity's greatness is mine. The infinite personality of man can only come from the magnificent harmony of all human races. My prayer is that India may represent the co-operation of all the people on this earth. For India unity is truth and division is evil.'

The poet's name is symbolic of the light of day, the sun which dispels the mists of darkness, the clouds of suspicion, and restores health to the human system.

Though his work was rooted in Indian soil his mind ranged over the wide world and his knowledge of human nature was deep. His work has, therefore, a universal appeal. His poems and songs vibrate with a peculiar passion which the pursuit of beauty aroused in him. They speak of the vicissitudes of friendship, the beauty of love, the pain of desolation, laughter and tears, terror and delight, the vanity of human wishes, the pains and heartaches of unfulfilled desires, the horror of moral obliquity, the shame of infamous conduct. They have the power of stirring our deepest emotions.

Rabindranath's writings have been translated into many languages but even the best translations do not bring out the music and the melody, the fire and the force of the original.

There is an unity of inspiration in Rabindranath's work. He was born at a time when India was in a revolutionary mood. There was a conscious revolt against social, political and religious institutions. Rabindranath participated in this movement and helped it forward. While he was aware of the social inadequacy and religious reaction and protested against them, he was deeply convinced of the validity and vitality of the fundamental ideals set forth by the seers and saints of India:

O Motherland! in thee the whole world takes delight.
First from thy forest-dwellings rose the sacred songs;
First from thy dawning spread the light
Of noble thoughts and deeds, in epic verses told.

India, he says, has saved through tumultuous ages, the living words that have issued from the illumined consciousness of her great seers. The genius of a few has touched the hearts of many.

In his poetry he gives personal endorsement to the classical tradition of India. When he loves India, it is this tradition that he loves. In his *Religion of Man* he writes: 'I do not consider India to be a geographical entity. To me it is spiritual personality. This is the spirit of faith in the metaphysical being of man which may perhaps exhaust all our material prosperity. Even after losing everything India stands steadfastly embracing that spirit. It is a glory sufficient to justify hope for its future.' In 1925, he brought out a book, *The Geographical Introduction to History*: 'There can be no play without a stage, no history without geography. Historical consciousness is revived in peoples' memories by association with certain places.'

Tagore's nationalism is internationalism. In a poem entitled *Pravasi* (The Emigrant) he writes:

My home is everywhere;
    I am in search of it;
My country is in all countries;
    I will struggle to attain it.

He asks us to measure ourselves against the achievements of our forefathers. Streams of men poured into the country in resistless tides from places unknown and were lost in the one sea of India. Aryans and Dravidians, Sakas and Huns, the Pathans and the Moghuls, these people of diverse origin influenced Indian culture which is one, though varied in its manifestations.

'To know my country, one has to travel to that age when she realized her soul and thus transcended her physical boundaries, when she revealed her being in a radiant magnanimity which illumined the eastern horizon, making her recognized as their own by those in alien shores who were awakened into a surprise of life, and not now when she has withdrawn herself into a narrow barrier of obscurity, into a misery of pride, of exclusiveness, into a poverty of mind that dumbly revolves around itself in an unmeaning repetition of a past that has lost its sight and has no message for the pilgrim of the future.'

Tagore's philosophy was one of wholeness and unity. He fought against the evil of division, of multiplicity.

The philosophic outlook of India inspired the writings of Rabindranath Tagore. Philosophy had no place in the original family of the Muses. Coleridge, however, considered it to be a twin genius to poetry. Discussing Shakespeare's poetry, Coleridge says: 'No man was ever yet a great poet without being at the same time a profound philosopher.' We find in Rabindranath the conjunction of a brilliant imagination and a passionate concern for conveying through his writings the basic intellectual and moral concepts of Indian culture. All ages of renaissance are ages when men suddenly discover the seed of thought in their ancient past. Rabindranath says: 'Emancipation from the bondage of the soil is no freedom for the tree.'

Goethe expresses the yearning of the human spirit through Faust: 'I have to know that the world contains in its inmost being.' Our present civilization in some of its aspects robs the world of its mystery, pretends to have an answer to every question and teaches us to believe that what can be seen, touched and measured alone is real. At a time when the heavens no longer declare the glory of God, but have become an eternal silence of infinite space, when the world is no longer seen as a field of Divine purpose but appears to obey blindly the laws of a mechanistic science, Rabindranath affirmed the reality of the Divine Spirit which informs and inspires the universe. The world is not the sum total of things that exist. It is not what is governed by laws.

Rabindranath understands the doubts and difficulties felt by the critics of religion. 'I am able to love my God because He gives me freedom to deny Him.' Many an atheist is seriously engaged in a creative search for the Divine. Atheism is not a negative denial of God but a positive movement of the spirit to reach the Divine behind the new dimensions of

74

reality which modern knowledge provides. Though knowledge has no limit, mystery has no end.

Dissatisfaction with the actual and yearning for the Beyond are the keynote of all religions. Man struggles to attain perfection. To fail to achieve it is no disgrace; to lack the desire for it is a misfortune. Man's struggle is for emancipation.

I am restless. I am athirst for far away things,
> My soul goes out in a longing to touch the skirt of the dim distance.

O Great Beyond, O the keen call of thy flute!
> I forget, I ever forget, that I have no wings to fly, that I am bound in this spot evermore.

Indian tradition believes that man has to grow from the intellectual to the spiritual level. An intellectual apprehension of the Divine is different from the spiritual realization of it. 'Perfect freedom lies in the harmony of relationship which we realize not through knowing but in being. Objects of knowledge maintain an infinite distance from us who are the knowers. For knowledge is not union. We attain the world of freedom only through perfect sympathy.' Tagore says, 'I have seen what is unsurpassable', in the spirit of the *Upanisad* writer:

vedaham etam purusam mahantam aditya-varnam
tamasah parastat

The poet writes: 'I have seen, have heard, have lived in the depths of the known, have felt the truth that exceeds all knowledge which fills my heart with wonder and I sing.' Freedom is reached by the attainment of truth. Ignorance is bondage; knowledge is deliverance.

The basic quality of his life and thought was determined by certain experiences he had. Standing one morning on the verandah of his house, seeing the sun rise behind the rich foliage of the garden trees, he had a vision of the beauty and joy of the universe. 'I suddenly felt as if some ancient mist had in a moment lifted from my sight and the morning light on the face of the world revealed an inner radiance of joy. The invisible screen of the commonplace was removed from all things, and all men and their ultimate significance were intensified in my mind...The unmeaning fragments lost their individual isolation and my mind revelled in the unity of a vision..I felt sure that some Being who comprehended me and my world was seeking His best expression in all my experiences, uniting them into an ever-widening individuality which is a spiritual work of art.' Rabindranath's religion is based on vision, experience rather than on knowledge.

The ultimate truth in man is not his intellect but the illumined consciousness which he acquires when he extends his sympathy across all barriers of caste and colour. He then realizes that all things are spiritually alive. The world is not alien to us. It is the habitation of Man's spirit. Every object in existence has something ineffable about it.

The experience of Reality which the great seers have is not capable of exact definition. So varied representations are given. These are fashioned by heart, intelligence and mind, *hrda manisa, manasa*, to use the words of the *Upanisad*.

na samdrse tisthati rupam asya
na caksusa pasyati kascamainam
harda manisa manasabhiklpto
ya etad vidur amrtas te bhavanti

Not within the field of vision stands this form,

    no one whatsoever sees him with the eye

By heart, by thought, by mind apprehended,

    they who know him become immortal.

The poet's religion has no place for any fixed doctrine. Religion is an endless adventure of man's entire being towards a truth which is revealed in this very quest. Truth is not the exclusive possession of any one individual or class or race or religion. The one Truth has m any faces, *bahuni mukhani ekam sat vipra bahudha vadanti.* The real is one; wise men speak of it in many ways. On the basis of such a view, India had been struggling for *sarva-dharma-samanvaya.* The variations are determined by the accidents of geography and history. The concepts of God are relative to our traditions and training. This emphasis on unity in diversity as against uniformity, has persisted for centuries in the Indian outlook. This view negates discord for unity, comprehends the differences. When differences become contradictions, conflicts arise. Tagore repudiates narrow, dogmatic, exclusive views of religion. It is wrong to think that certain nations, certain races and certain creeds are specially chosen by God.

In his essay on *The Centre of Indian Culture,* Tagore says: 'We should remember that the doctrine of special creation is out of date, and the idea of a specially favoured race belongs to a barbaric age. We have come to understand that any special truth or special culture which is wholly dissociated from the universal is not true at all.' He reminds us that, 'Our forefathers did spread a single white carpet whereon all the world was cordially invited to take its seat in amity and good fellowship. No quarrel could have arisen there, for He in whose name the invitation went forth, for all time to come, was the Peaceful, in the heart of all conflicts; the God who is revealed through all losses and sufferings; the One in all diversities of creation. And in His name was this eternal truth declared in ancient India. He alone sees, who sees all beings in himself.'

Tagore looks upon the Supreme as personal. He writes: 'I was born in a family which, at that time, was earnestly developing a monotheistic religion based on the philosophy of the *Upanisads*.' Monotheism puts at the centre not a cold abstration cut off from the world but the Lord of Love who informs and inspires the universe.

As a poet Rabindranath is interested not in the Transcendent One but in its varied expressions. In an address which he gave on his seventieth birthday he said: 'The messengers of Truth's white Radiance, who purify earth, air and water, who guide men to the paths of peace, I honour them — and I know I am not of their company. But when that one Radiance throws itself out joyously this universal movement, then and there I find my vocation — as a poet. I am a voice of the expressive many, the Infinite's self-revelation, its endless, nameless joy, the passion of bliss that fathers forth all things.'

For Tagore, God, man and nature are bound together in single unity. He repudiates the view which looks upon the world as a valley of dry bones, a charnel-house, a sham, a lie. In medieval Europe, the flesh was treated as impure and the world as vanity and renunciation was prescribed as the only way to salvation. For Tagore the whole universe is a manifestation of the Supreme, *Isavasyam idam sarvam*. All things are interrelated in God, *sutre mani-gana iva*. Spirit and life are two poles of one Reality. When the world is enveloped by God, its pettiness is relieved. Tagore agrees with Pascal who says that 'a man does not show his greatness by being at one extremity, but rather by touching both at once.'

Even Samkara who is reputed to be the formulator of the maya doctrine did not look upon the world as a mere illusion or a dream. He tells us that it is evident to the whole world, *sarva-loka-pratyaksa*, that it is established by all experience, *sarvanubhava-sidha*.

For Tagore the world is various, beautiful, and new. It brings certitude and peace to the human soul. The poet affirms life, and without such an affirmation, life contradicts itself and denies its own existence. Life is essentially worth living. It may have its moments of pain and sorrow but it is valuable because of these things and the rewards which even a glimpse of self-knowlege brings. It is not right to think that only those who are uphappy can understand the sufferings of others. When we help others out of deep sympathy, our desire to help is rooted in the joy we feel in life. Unhappy people sometimes become embittered and want others to suffer also.

Human beings are born to love and be loved. The symbol used in India is the lotus and not the Cross, though both stress different aspects of the way to perfection. Tagore believes in man's capacity for joy and of his power to live in harmony with the natural and universal forces that surround him. 'The current of the world has its boundaries, otherwise it would have no existence, but its power is not shown in the boundaries that restrain it but in its movement which is towards perfection.'

Religion is not to be confused with doctrinal conformity or ceremonial piety. It is the purification of the soul, the remaking of self. It is not a mere quest of truth but a conquest of our selfishness, pride, greed, etc. It is through self-control that man can reach his goal. The extinction of the ego is the way to fulfilment. Progress towards the goal is through continual sacrifice. 'Life,' says Rabindranath, 'is an eternal sacrifice at the altar of death.'

When we grow into the image of the Divine, when we dwell in Him and with Him, we become channels of His light and power, instruments of His working. He only knows the truth who knows the unity of all beings in the spirit. Then all men are seen as brothers: *bhrataro manavas sarve*. This is the root principle of Indian culture, its *mulamantra*, for human beings are the rays of the Divine, sparks of the Supreme Spirit, *mamaivamso jiva loke jivabhutah sanatanah*.

For Tagore there is no conflict between social aims and spiritual life. The title which he gave to his Hibbert Lectures was — *The Religion of Man*. It is the religion of all humanity. All human beings share a common destiny in a universe whose mystery still remains unfathomed. He has a sensitive social conscience. When he referred to the evil days on which the country had fallen, he emphasized the social inadequacies, the humiliations and hardships to which millions of our countrymen were subjected. We are all born equal but we are made unequal by the way we are brought up. Reverence for personality is the central principle of all ethics. In our practice we have overlooked it. Tagore rebelled against orthodoxies, clashes of castes and creeds and indifference to the disinherited of the earth.

My head is bowed in sorrow

My eyes keep back their tears

My heart is rent by this reproach.

Political development is inseparable from moral development. Our political bondage is a symptom of our inward weakness. 'They who have failed to attain swaraj within themselves must lose it in the outside world too.' He demanded a positive programme of national reconstruction and not a mere rejection of foreign rule. We must remove the internal causes which give rise to social and political instability. He was an optimist with reference to India's future.

The poet is not a dreamer or a visionary. He keeps constant vigil over the world. He is the great sentinel, as Gandhi called him. The moral health of a nation depends on the inspiration the people derive from their poets and artists.

Asceticism for Rabindranath is self-control and not abstention from worldly activities. Very early in his life, when he was hardly seventeen, he had the need to control his emotions and his aphorism indicates his attitude.

The fire restrained in the tree
    Fashions flowers;
Released from bonds it dies in ashes.

He was sensitive to the beauty of women. In his poem The *Bridegroom*, he says :

Because you and ·I shall meet
    The heavens are full of light,
Because you and I shall meet
    The world is full of greenery.

Self-knowledge is not intended to seduce us from activity directed towards the outside world to an exclusive contemplativeness. Man knows himself insofar as he knows the world. To know oneself as separate is untruth; or realize one's unity with the universe is to know the truth. God-realization brings us into close relationship with the world of men and the universe. It does not take us away from life. 'My heart throbs to mingle with the heart of humanity. Some seek wisdom, others wealth, but I seek thy company so that I may sing.' Tagore does not believe in a sheltered life. In one of his poems in *Gitanjali* he says: 'Our Master himslf has joyfully taken upon Him the bonds of creation. He is bound with us all for ever.'

Goethe says: 'In the beginning was the deed'. In the name of spiritual freedom, we should not retreat from action. Austerity is not inaction. 'The householder shall have his life established in Brahma, shall pursue the deeper truth of all things and in all activities of life, dedicate his works to the Eternal Being. Thus we have come to know that what India truly seeks is not a peace which is negation or some mechanical adjustment, but that which is in *sivam* (God), in goodness, which is in truth of perfect union; that India does not enjoin her children to cease from *Karma* (action) but to perform their karma in the presence of the Eternal, with the pure knowledge of the spiritual meaning of existence. India has two aspects — in one she is a householder; in the other a wandering ascetic. The former refuses to budge from the home corner, the latter has no home at all. I find both these within me. I want to roam about and see all the wide world, yet I also yearn for a little sheltered nook; like a bird with its tiny nest for a dwelling, and the vast sky for flight.'

Tagore did not believe in a life-denying asceticism. 'India has not split up her dharma by setting apart one side of it for practical and the other for ornamental purposes. Dharma in India is religion for the whole of society — its roots reach deep underground, but its top touches the Heaven alike, overspreading the whole life of man, like a gigantic banyan tree. To realize the One in the universe and also in our own inner nature, to set up that One amidst diversity, to discover it by means of knowledge, to perceive it by means of Love and to preach it by means of conduct — this is the work that India has been doing in spite of many obstacles and calamities, in ill success and good fortune alike.'

Those who expected to find an unworldly saint in Tagore were greatly surprised by his tough earthly quality. Saints are expected to live normal, balanced lives. The *Mahabharata* says: *Dharmartha kamah samam evasevyah ya ekasevi sanaro jaghanyah.* The ideals of social life, economic pursuits and the enjoyment of beauty should be cultivated equally; he who is devoted to only one of these has an impoverished life. An image used in Indian religious classics is familiar to all. Water surrounds the lotus flower but does not wet its petals. Even so human individuals should work in the world without being affected by it. Tagore himself was a harmonious man in whom there was a happy blend of contemplation and action.

In *A Poet's Testament*, Rabindranath confesses: 'I have completed seventy years of my life but even now my friends complain of the trait of frivolity which interferes with the gravity becoming to old age. I am afraid I cannot afford to be more serious. Those who want to place me on a high pedestal, with the ringing of bells and the sounding of conchshells, to them I would say, "I have been born in a lower rung...I am a poet and nothing else".'

When people celebrated his birthday he told them: 'Do not remind me of my age by celebrating my birthdays. I refuse to believe that age has anything to do with my life which knows nothing but the immortal youthfulness in which I am one with my *jivandevata*, the God of my life.' Youth is not a period of life. It is a state of mind, a quality of emotions, a temper of the spirit. We do not grow old by living a certain number of years. We grow old if we lose our ideals, if we become immune to change. Years may wrinkle the skin; the soul is wrinkled if we give up love and loyalty. Whether we are twenty or seventy, we are young so long as we have in our heart the spirit of wonder, of curiosity, the challenge to life and joy in adventure. This is the meaning of the saying that we are as young as we feel.

Rabindranath emphasizes the uniqueness of man. Man is within nature and yet understands nature. He is the only organism where life has become conscious of itself. He is gifted with imagination, with reason, with awareness of his existence, of his death and of all the many choices he has to make. He is torn away from the primitive harmony which the animal has in its relation to nature. He needs to relate himself to others, to the world; if he does not, he feels insecure.

'God,' Rabindranath says, 'has many strings to his *sitar*; some are made of iron, others of copper, and yet others are made of gold. Humanity is the golden string of God's lute. His freedom, his ethical and aesthetic consciousness make man the golden string.' In the preface to his collected works, Rabindranath says, 'This world I have loved; Greatness I have saluted; Freedom I have aspired for and I have believed that Man is true and that Universal Man is ever living in the heart of the people.'

When it is said that man is moulded by history Rabindranath demurs as an artist. He is alone as a creator. He is not caught in the toils of outward events. In one of his letters to his daughter written in 1927, Tagore says: '...within the depths of our soul, there is a place for eternal peace, where our eternal slaves exist beyond the births and deaths, the unions and separations, the gains and losses of the world. If we can make room for ourselves there, then we really live; earthly living is not living at all.' The soul is the creator; all others are the material for creation. The materials may come from history, from social environment. They do not create the human being. He expresses himself through them. The living spirit in us liberates us from the mechanism of compulsion. It is freedom that helps us to order our life and move forward in the education of the human race. Great sources of knowledge and deep wells of inspiration are available to us so that we may select worthy goals and work effectively for realizing them. We have the power to change the course of history. Things do not happen in an inevitable way. Even materialists who affirm in theory that man is determined to behave as though they had decisions to make and it is important for them to make decisions. Man has the power to set himself against the environment and retain his dignity.

At a time when technique has become all-important, the existentialists protest against the resulting emptiness, meaninglessness of life, anxiety, split consciousness, disintegration of the self. Darwin's theory of evolution, Freud's insistence on the unconscious and the manipulations of conditioned reflexes to social and psychological engineering all tend to reduce man to the status of an object. Science, cannot reduce to mere objects, the discoverers of the marvels of science and their application. We must take into account all dimensions of man.

Each individual can contribute to the progressive life of humanity by perfecting his own nature, by liberating himself from the compulsions of nature and the restraints of history.

Rabindranath believed in the creative value of human freedom and in the validity of reason as a guide against dogmatism. The present trend toward the extinction of the individual is a serious portent for the future of civilization. The mobilization of human beings, in war as in peace, as instruments for realizing the will of a dictator or a ruling group, dehumanizes man. For Tagore whatever promotes and enhances life is good; whatever injures and cramps life is evil.

In his essay on *Society and State*, Tagore says: 'Do not distrust your own strength; know for certain that the great hour has come. Know for certain that a unifying power has always worked in India. Even in the most adverse circumstances India has always worked her way out; that is why India still survives. I believe in this India. Even today, at this very moment, this India is slowly and surely building up a wonderful consistency between her ancient traditions and the modern times. Let each of us do his share consciously; let not mutinous feelings or sheer stupidity make us un-co-operative at every turn.' Again, 'The forces that lie locked within us must find release under the stress of foreign onslaught, for today the world stands sorely in need of the priceless gifts which the ancient rishis of India earned by their self-discipline. Providence will not let these gifts go to waste. That is why, in the fullness of time, He has roused us by this agony of suffering.' The spiritual legacy of the past should be distinguished from the dead encumbrances. From the altar we must take the fire and not the ashes of dead forms. Rabindranath gives us many stories of wasted lives, anguished hearts, broken relationships resulting from submission to orthodox beliefs.

Religion, if it is not to fade away, should undergo a radical transformation. Ancient dogmas do not touch our hearts or satisfy our minds. Forms that were adapted to situations and issues that no longer exist require to be changed. Our doubts have dimensions deeper than we realize.

Rabindranath was an organ of national life. He composed the National Anthem. It was sung for the first time at the Indian National Congress in 1911. It is a song in praise of the land with its hills and rivers, and with its many peoples, races and religions, all to be woven in a garland of love. It is a stirring appeal to unity under the Creator, the Dispenser of India's destiny, *bharata-bhagya-vidhata*. The words kindle in the heart of man, the sense of unity of oneself with all and brings the hearts of all people into the harmony of one life.

Though Rabindranath was essentially a literary artist, his voice was raised whenever grave injustices were committed. When evil is perpetrated, we have an obligation to speak out and act against it. Tagore along with Gandhi, was responsible for the awakening of the national spirit and all through his life he was as much against the cowardice of the weak as against the arrogance of the strong. In his patriotism there was no trace of hatred, bitterness or chauvinism.

When the Sedition Bill was passed in 1898 and the great leader Tilak was arrested, Tagore raised his voice against the repressive policy of the Government and actively participated in raising funds for Tilak's defence.

When Bengal was partitoned in 1905,[1] Tagore was greatly disturbed. He poured out songs full of the spirit of nationalism. 'There is no salvation for man if the power of the weak is not awakened at once, because the weapon of the powerful has exceeded its limits; the helplessness of the weak knows no bounds today; all opportunities and advantages are heaped on one side of human society while helplessness reigns supreme on the other.'

When the Jallianwala Bagh[2] attrocities occurred, he returned his knighthood and wrote a letter to the Viceroy, Lord Chelmsford, which concluded with the words, 'The time has come when badges of honour make our shame glaring in their incongruous context of distinctions, by the side of those of my countrymen who, for their so-called insignificance, are liable to suffer a degradation not fit for human beings.'

For Tagore, as for Gandhi, the measure of man's greatness is not his material possessions, but the truth in him which is universal. Hatred is more deadly than violence. It is an outrage on humanity. Man's strength lies in mercy and compassion. When Gandhi started the non-co-operation movement,[3] Tagore thought that it was a kind of political asceticism. He was not attracted to negation, emptiness, even as a temporary expedient. He tried his best to understand the positive side of the non-co-operation movement but failed. 'And I say to myself, if you cannot keep step with your countrymen at this great crisis of their history, never say that you are right and the rest of

---

[1]Under the recommendation of Lord Curzor, Bengal was divided in 1905, creating a new province of East Bengal.

[2]A walled garden in Amritsar, where people celebrating the festival of *Baisakh* on April 13, 1919, were continously fired upon by troops on orders of Brigadier General R.E.H.Dyer, killing 379 persons and wounding 1200, including women and children.

[3]1920-22, marked the first country-wide mass compaign against British rule.

87

them wrong; only give up your role as a soldier, go back to your corner as poet; be ready to accept popular derision and disgrace.'

The Second World War disturbed him a great deal. When Miss Eleanor Rathbone appealed to Tagore to persuade India to come openly into the war against the Nazis, he pointed out how India herself had no political freedom. In his address on *The Crisis of Civilization* which he wrote a few weeks before his death, Tagore asks us to crusade for a civilization in which peace would be possible. Only an ethical movement can rescue us from the spirit of barbarism which has corrupted our civilization and is breeding wars and more destructive wars.

Rabindranath's prayer for his country is, 'Let the promises and hopes, the deeds and words of my country be true, my Lord.' He does not say 'my country, right or wrong' but prays that his country may always adopt the right line of conduct.

Though he criticized British rule and worked for the country's liberation from British domination, he had no hatred for the British. In a letter to Mr.C.F. Andrews in 1921, Tagore wrote: 'With all our grievances against the English nation, I cannot help loving your country, which has given me some of my dearest friends. I am intensely glad of this fact, for it is hateful to hate. The fact is that the best people in all countries find their affinity with one another. The fuel displays its differences but the fire is one. When the fire comes before my vision in this country I recognize it as the same thing which lights our path in India and illuminates our house. Let us seek that fire and know that wherever the spirit of separation is supreme, there reigns darkness. Let me light my own lamp with love for the great humanity revealed in your country.'

Civilization cannot sustain itself on violence. It is not judged by the power it develops but by the love and humanity it evolves. The causes which bring about the decay and decline of civilizations are callousness of heart, softening of moral fibre, cheapening of man's worth and enslavement of men by machines. Mankind can save itself from destruction only by a renewal of spiritual values. The creative individual should work with energy combined with patience. Man's greatness consists in his decision to be more powerful than his condition.

India's history is not a separate exclusive history of either the Hindus or the Muslims. 'Those Muslims,' Rabindranath said, 'who throughout the ages and since so many generations had made the soil of this land their own, by births and deaths — they too have a place in the history of India.' Even the British have become a part of our history.

'Let the awakening of the East drive us consciously to discover the essential and universal meaning in our own civilization, to remove the debris from its path, to rescue it from its bondage of stagnation that produces impurities, to make it a great channel of communication between all human races.'

There is something in Rabindranath's teaching that is not of this earth. He was concerned with the invisible spirit of man, with the profundities and not the trivialities of life. He asks us to cling to ultimate common sense in the confusion of life. He believed in regeneration through love and suffering. He was not afraid of change. If emphasis on social reconstruction is treated as a Western value, the work of Rabindranath Tagore illustrates how Western values could be integrated with Eastern ideals. His songs are sung and his verses are remembered. His voice was the conscience of our age. He became a spokesman and a guide for his generation. He bequeathed to his country and the world, a life which had no littleness about it.

SARDAR VALLABHBHAI PATEL

— ॐ —

A courageous rebel, a wise statesman and
a model administrator.

We may look upon Sardar Patel's life in three parts — a rebel, a statesman, an administrator. Until we attained freedom, he was a disciplined soldier carrying out the behests of his leader, Mahatma Gandhi. In whatever he did, he carried out Gandhiji's wishes. Even when he differed from him, he subordinated his personal inclinations to the commands of the general whose mandate he was carrying out. In Borsad, Bardoli, and in several battles of freedom, he was in the front rank. Everywhere he acted with great discipline. He never put his interests higher than those of the nation.

He was a man of few words. He possessed clarity, conviction and prudence. He belonged to an agricultural family and showed his deep interest in the welfare of the peasants. The campaigns which he organized under the leadership of Mahatma Gandhi were all intended to bring together the people of the localities concerned, to bind them together, to make them have one single purpose, to make them subordinate their caste and communal differences and work as one whole. That is the task which yet requires to be done.

The most important part of his work was as a statesman. Immediately after the achievement of freedom, in a period of two years, by skilful handling, by persuasive power, he integrated over 500 states into the Indian Union. As Prime Minister Nehru said, 'Sardar Patel is the architect of India's unity.' Through his persuasive power, diplomatic skill, political adroitness, he was able to bring about the administrative unity of this country, which is the essential base for building up a strong India. This administrative unification has to be transformed into emotional integration and national cohesion. We have been trying to do it all these years.

What this country would have been without such integration is hard to imagine. Even after this integration, today we are still asking for integration and solidarity. Look at the provinces. Look at the different parts of the country where communal differences, caste animosities, are still dominating our public affairs. You find distinctions such as Kamma and Reddy, Lingayat and Vokkaligars, Kayasth and Rajput — these differences are still there. What is needed today is a complete integration of our country. We may belong to this caste or that religion; but that must be regarded as a very subordinate aspect and purely personal affair of the individual. That should not be brought into public affairs. Our history in recent times has been marred by the exaggerated attachment we give to these things. We must look upon ourselves as Indians first and foremost. The countries which have made the greatest progress even in the East are Japan and China. There are Muslims there, there are Christians there, there are Buddhists there; but no one thinks of these things when the interests of the nation are involved. Everyone looks upon himself as a Japanese or a Chinese. Here in our country we still regard ourselves as belonging to this community or that caste and these differences dominate, vitiate and pollute our social structure.

It is, therefore, essential that the integration of the States which Sardar started must be continued until we all feel that we belong to one nation. That is the integration which we are still aiming at.

About the achievement of Sardar in this matter, I remember a comment made by a London daily – 'This will stand out as a great historic achievement by Sardar Patel on a level with Bismarck, if not higher.' That is what the *London Times* said when he died.

He was a courageous patriot, a man of great wisdom in administration. I remember that three of our great leaders at one time were Chairmen of three different municipalities, or corporations as they are called today. Rajen Babu was the Chairman of Patna Municipality; Jawaharlal Nehru was Chairman of Allahabad Municipality; and Sardar Patel was Chairman of Ahmedabad Municipality. Their selfless labours and their organizing skill were known to all people. Now we have achieved this administrative unification. Something more needs to be done if our country is to become a first-class power, and not become a second-class or third-class power: complete coherence and integration, subordination of our minor differences to the one great concept of India as a living part of humanity. In the Independence pledge it is said that the British brought on us a four-fold disaster – political, economic, cultural and spiritual. Now that we have assumed control over the country, it is these four we have to demolish.

As an administrator, when floods overtook Gujarat, when he organized the Bardoli campaign, in all the other spheres where he worked he showed great organizing ability. He was the Chairman of the Ahmedabad Municipality and made it into a modern one. People did not talk then of leakage and wastage of public funds. They were all sure that everything collected would be usefully spent for the purpose for which it was intended. Today, there is so much talk of corruption. It may be true or it may not be true. But that there should be such talk is a reflection on our general character and ability. Therefore, we as administrators must see to it that we do not give any room or scope for criticism of that type. People who administer a great country like ours must be above suspicion, must be able to risk their lives, if necessary, for the sake of the country and not pander to the whims or the pressures of society. That is very necessary.

The economic standards will have to be raised. Unless we fight the demon of poverty which is responsible ultimately for caste and communal differences, unless we are able to bring down hunger, unemployment and disease, we will not be able to raise the economic standards of our people. So the root cause of all our troubles — caste trouble, communal trouble, low caste, Harijan, touchable, untouchable — may be ultimately traced to the extreme poverty from which most of our people suffer. If we are able to raise the level of the living standards of our people, this suffering will not continue. Not only are standards necessary, each individual is a keystone in the arch of this country. Our people are the most valuable asset which we possess, and unless we are able to give them some kind of cultural outlook, some sense of belonging to a great nation which has had great traditions, our education will not be regarded in any sense as complete.

People generally say that they do not believe in religion. There is scepticism in matters of belief; there is a lack of guides so far as our moral conduct is concerned; and there is no sense of values. Religion is not something which is an aside or a parenthesis. It is the deepest part of our being. In all our activities, if we live from the dimension of depth, we are religious. The Infinite or Supreme is the deepest part of our being. We must work not on the surface but from the ultimate depths. Life from depth is authentically a religious life. If you are able to give to your children that kind of outlook, they will not be carried away by the sophistications and the scepticism of the modern world. We will all become really, deeply, authentically, religious in our nature.

The defence of democracy, the defence of the moral values with which democracy is bound up, the raising of the living standards of our people, the giving of a proper cultural outlook to our young men and women as also the giving to them a sense of depth in their relations with their neighbours — that is what we aim at; and it is my earnest hope that in this country we will have this proper orientation.

A life like Sardar Patel's reminds us of the self-sacrificing labours of one of the great makers of modern India. His devotion to duty, his disciplined obedience, his courage and his preparedness to throw away his life — these are all qualities which we have to learn from his example.

He was one of the pivotal figures in our recent history both before and after the achievement of freedom.

During the struggle for our freedom he was a loyal lieutenant of Mahatmaji — Gandhiji's word was a law to him, and under his guidance conducted the Civil Resistance Campaigns in Borsad and Bardoli. He asked the peasants of Bardoli to challenge the Government to take their lands to England. Bardoli became the sign of hope and symbol of strength of the Indian peasants under proper leadership. Observing his work in Bardoli, Gandhiji remarked: 'Vallabhbhai found his Vallabh God in Bardoli.'

Already references have been made to his work of integrating the states and bringing the 500 and odd states into the framework of Central administration. Patel realized that the political stability of the country was bound up with its unity.

How smoothly the work was done is illustrated by the fact that the Maharaja Saheb of Gwalior, who was himself affected by this process of integration, has paid tribute to the vision and work of Sardar Patel. Anyone who encourages fissiparous tendencies in our country is no friend of the country. We must develop that social solidarity which transcends the bonds of kinship, caste and religion.

Patel was successful in implementing his ideas; for in any Committee he who knows his mind will always prevail over others who approach the problems with open and sometimes blank minds. He always knew what he meant to do and he did it. Firmness and decision were his characteristics.

He could be angry though he rarely lost his temper. He was never self-righteous. He had no personal fads or conventional prejudices. He had an acute sense of the past, a critical appreciation of what in it had vitality and power of survival. Life must be understood backwards and lived forwards. We should not cling to the past. In politics as in life, it is silly to cry for the last month's moon.

Revolutions generally leave a trail of disappointment and disillusionment behind them. In the excitement of the struggle we proclaim great ideals and entertain high hopes. Where the struggle is over we are brought into contact with hard reality and the attempt to apply these ideals leads to compromises, retreats which tarnish the purity of the achievement. Every successful revolution faces criticism not only from the right, from its dispossessed victims, but also from the left, from its one-time supporters who accuse it of having betrayed its principles. What is essential is to hold fast to the ideals, the fundamental principles which govern the revolution.

Some of us regard ourselves as innately good but betrayed by circumstances. It is better to discern signs of inward decay and check them in time. No outside country can degrade a nation. It could be degraded only by itself. We must try to see to it that in every act we do, we behave as worthy descendants of the great leaders who placed the service of the people above all other considerations.

Government exists for the millions and the leaders must be in close touch with the needs and aspirations, fears and apprehensions of the common people. They cannot afford to live in unnatural isolation from the people's minds and spirits. Sardar Patel left an example of freedom through disciplined obedience. The freedom has to be continually re-earned by service and sacrifice.

In Sardar Patel we had a great courageous rebel, a wise statesman and a model administrator. If we remember these qualities of Sardar Vallabhbhai Patel, our country will steadily progress. It is my earnest hope that these great qualities of his will inspire us in the future.

DR. RAJENDRA PRASAD

— ॐ —

Embodiment of that what is best in Indian culture.

I t is the good fortune of this country that in the formative
years of our Republic, immediately after the establishment
of the Republic, Dr. Prasad was elected President and that he
guided the destinies of our country for over 12 years. He was
the embodiment of what is best in Indian culture. The peaks
of our achievement are symbolized by service, renunciation
and sacrifice. These three qualities were embodied in him. His
life, from the time he entered the national struggle down to the
last day of his life, was devoted to the service of this country.

It is true that he took a leading part in many other activities,
too. But here we are concerned with his work for the
development of the Constitution and the work which he did
for human fellowship. The last address which he gave in
Delhi was at the Anti-nuclear Convention. As a true disciple
of Gandhiji, he made out that we should try to avoid every
kind of violence, that we should struggle to establish peace
and friendship among nations; and he formulated a proposal

for unilateral nuclear disarmament. Even though it may have appeared to be utopian when he formulated it, it is an ideal to which the whole world looks forward.

It was in his lifetime that nuclear developments arose. There were the methods of the past, battles, violent struggles, etc. But when these had taken place, we could still survive as they affected only parts of the world, not the whole of it. Nuclear armaments and nuclear warfare mean the destruction of all the civilized values for which we stand. The methods of the past cannot be regarded as applicable to the present. So, even though we may consider that what he suggested was utopian, yet that is the only thing that can give the human community stability, poise and balance.

We cannot merely ask for nuclear disarmament. We must remove the causes that cause wars. The causes are mutual fear, distrust, animosities and the feeling of insecurity among nations. If we are to survive in this world as peaceful nations, these causes have to be removed. Men must feel that humanity is one whole, irrespective of caste or community, class or race. They must try to widen the horizon of their understanding, advance in knowledge, grow in grace and feel that when one individual in one part of the country or the world suffers, all others do suffer.

Dr. Rajendra Prasad, as a faithful disciple of Gandhiji, argued for human fellowship. It is one of the things inscribed in our Constitution. We stand for political justice and freedom, fraternity and fellowship. This is one of the remarkable objectives of our Constitution. We cannot achieve it unless we advance towards it step by step. Many of the things that we do may appear to be very rash from the practical point of view today but ultimately it is the steps that seem to be impossible and it is the push of the impossible that makes the world a place in which we can live with some kind of amity and friendship.

Rajen Babu held this ideal and the last address he gave to the Delhi people, to the country and the world at large, was the one on unilateral nuclear disarmament. Not that it is going to be realized tomorrow or the day after, but he knew for certain that if this world was to become a happy home, if people were to live together in amity and friendship, that was the only way. We must cease to hate each other; we must cease to have hostilities; we must love one another and try to develop understanding of one another. It is this ideal that possessed him and he made the proposal even though he was certain that many in his audience would not accept the rationale of it.

I would like to say that he was a faithful disciple of Gandhiji. He was a believer in democracy which he thought, was a progressive system. What exists today in the name of democracy cannot be regarded as satisfactory. It is something which is perpetually moving forward; if it does not move forward, it is not democracy. It must go on until it embraces the whole world and makes it a happy human community.

ACHARYA SHRI TULSI

— ॐ —

The human side of true progress.

Acharya Shri Tulsi was the head of the order of *Terapanths*[1] for over twenty five years. It has a large number of monks and lakhs of laymen. The great respect which they all had for Acharya Tulsiji was a sign of his outstanding personality.

Acharya Shri Tulsi's impact on the Indian community was due to the *anuvrat* movement which he had started. There was a general feeling in the country that while we were attending to the material progress and doing substantial work in that direction, we were neglecting the human side of true progress. A civilized human being must be free from greed, vanity, passion, anger. Civilizations decline if there is a coarsening of moral fibre, if there is callousness of heart. Man is tending to becoming a robot, a mechanical instrument caring for nothing except his material welfare, incapable of exercising his intelligence and responsibility. He seems to prefer comfort to liberty, our politicians, resorting to direct action to enforce

---

[1]Jain monks and nuns, belonging to *Svetambara* sect.

their particular viewpoint or to fulfil their desires. This is unfortunate and to remedy this growing indiscipline, lack of rectitude and egotism the *anuvrat* movement was started on March 1, 1949. It required strict adherence to the principles of the good life. It was intended to impart education in moral and spiritaul values.

We cannot say that, as a result of this movement, things have improved very considerably. Public spirit, commercial integrity, individual rectitude, family life, peaceful behaviour, these require to be cultivated. These cannot be achieved by merely talking about them. The only way in which this can be brought about is by imparting to our young people the essentials of our culture. These may be summarized in the three great words — *abhaya, ahimsa, asanga* — which are the common possessions of all systems of religious thought.

Abhaya — the world in which we live is full of suffering: *lakam soka hatam ca samastani* — disease, old age, death — the *Upanisads* raise this question and asks whether there is a way out of it and believes that there is. The Buddha speaks in a similar way; so does Christianity. The *Gita* affirms — *anityam asukham lokam* — and argues that we can get rid of these troubles by the worship of the Divine. Thus we get the Ultimate Reality. *Brahma-jijñasa* is the love of wisdom. The only way of getting rid of fear is by the conviction that there is something which redeems us from this world of time; something timeless. The *Upanisads* say: *anandam brahmano vidvan na bibheti kadacana*. The writer of the *Gita* says: *ma sucah* — be not afraid. The Buddha says that if we follow the ethical path, there will be an end of suffering.

Simply because we are afraid, it does not follow that there is something which removes our fear. Simply because we are hungry, it does not follow that there is food which will appease our hunger. The assumption of a Transcendent Reality may merely be a wish fulfilment. So it is argued that we should take an empirical survey of the world and by means of reason establish the Reality of something timeless and transcendent. Brahman is the world-ground.

A mere wish or a logical conclusion is not enough. We must have an encounter, a personal experience of the Supreme. Faith is not belief, but a state of the soul. All the systems believe in this. The Bodhi of the Buddha, the *Kevala Jñana*, the *Samyog darsana* of the Jain, the integrated insight, the *Brahmasāmsparsa* of the *Gita*, Truth which casts out fear, of the Christians — these all depend on personal realization.

The peculiarity of Indian systems of thought is that this insight into Reality means the discovery of the Divine in us. The *Chandogya Upanisad* says that truth by which this whole world is sustained is in the human being — *etad atmayam idam sarvam tat satyam sa atma tat twam asi*. Again, *esa devo visvakarma matatma sada jananam hrdaye sannivistah-deho devalayo nama*.

The Buddha's medications are an endeavour to know the highest. The Jains believe that behind the body of Karma, there is in each soul infinite knowledge, infinite power, infinite happiness. The *jiva* is by its very nature pure. Ultimate knowledge is its inherent possession. It is overlaid by ignorance created by the karmic body. When dwelling within the bonds of karma, the *jiva* experiences only finite knowledge, but as the impediments to greater knowledge are removed, infinite knowledge is manifested and the true nature of the soul is revealed. The impediments are desires and passions.

The perfected soul is *sidha paramesthin*. It is a state of unconditioned being, passionless peace, dissociated from desire and action. The *arhat* has not reached ultimate liberation but works in the world with compassion for it. Then we have ordinary human teachers.

From this follows a kind of hospitality to all religious creeds.

ajo'pi sann avyayatma bhutanam isvaro'pi san prakrtim
svam adhisthaya sambhavamy atmamayaya.

Though (I am) unborn, my self is imperishable, though I am the Lord of all creation, yet establishing myself in my own nature, I come into (empiric) being through my power. *Syadvada* affirms that the absolute of experience is not the absolute of language or of logic. We should not quarrel about the names we give to the Supreme or the ways by which we greet Him. On the wings of aspiration, man rises from earth to heaven, from ignorance to knowledge, from darkness to light. Without this aspiration man remains pruely animal, earthly, sensual, unenlightened and uninspired.

Ahimsa — If we believe that each individual has the Divine in him, it follows that our attitude towards others should be one of non-injury. *Ahimsa* is *vaira tyaga* — renunciation of hatred. There is no question that all those who are free from fear, who have attained *abhaya* will act in the world in a spirit of love and compassion — *karuna*. Love is the basis of all civilized living. All our unhappiness is traceable to our insatiable selfishness. Suffering is the result of craving, of greed. Our life will be suffering and our end sorrow, until we overcome our selfishness. *Marana* is not extinction. It is the extinction of craving which makes life mean and pitiful. It is serenity of soul. The Buddha says: 'To those in need give without restraint.' *Tyaga* or renunciation is the way to it. Not by giving up vain clothing or outward riches, not by abstaining from certain foods, but by giving up the spirit of vanity, the desire for wealth, the lust for self-indulgence, by giving up hatred, jealousy and selfishness, do we attain purity of heart. The man of passion is eager to put others right, the man of wisdom puts himself right. Self-conquest means self-liberation. *Triratna* of the Jains is faith, right knowledge and right conduct. The *pancasila* of the Jains is *ahimsa, satya, asteya, brahmacarya, aparigraha,* and of the Buddhists is practically the same, *ahimsa, satyavacana, brahmacarya, aparigraha and surapana-nisedha.*

Asanga — While we work in this world, we do so free from any attachment to the results of action, *yogasthah kuru karmani sangam tyaktva dhananjaya.* Again, *gata sangasya muktasya. Muktah* is free from *sanga.* We are unattached but not uninterested.

If we are able to spread these essentials of spiritual life, freedom from fear, love and non-attachment, we will improve the character of human beings. *Anuvrat Sangha* which Acharya Tulsiji has established, and is working for, aims at this moral improvement of the individual and, therefore, of society.

A true democracy has for its aim the making of moral personalities. Political power in a democracy is attained by appeals to people through the Press and the platform. Moral power, on the other hand, resides in a moral personality and in the latter's compelling characteristic. There is always this difference between the King and the Prophet, Rama and Vasistha, the political and the spiritual power. The desire for power is 'the perpetual and restless desire of power that ceaseth only in death', in the words of Hobbes. Its end is enslavement and its sanction force and the manipulation of society for personal greed. Spiritual leaders speak of the soul and the health of the soul; they utter words that provoke, stimulate, awaken; they are not objects of knowledge but stimulants to thought, ungraspable but always beckoning us. These we should hold before us in all our activities.

MAULANA ABUL KALAM AZAD

— ॐ —

Profound humanism, a civilized mind.

Maulana Abul Kalam was an outstanding figure of great courage, fearlessness, integrity and passionate love for freedom. He was a unique figure in our political life for nearly two generations. Even before he joined the Congress in 1920, he was a revolutionary. His political wisdom, patriotic fervour and sacrificial service were recognized early and he was made the President of the Indian National Congress in 1923, a position which he held for a number of years on different crucial occasions. His services to the country as a sagacious statesman, an ardent patriot, and a great intellectual are inestimable. He suffered for his convictions, but he never shrank from expressing his views. Among the great qualities of leadership he had was this: that he never shrank from expressing his views for fear of losing his popularity. A leader has to be firm. No man can be a leader if he does not risk unpopularity for his views. He who tries to please all, ends by pleasing none.

Maulana Azad noticed the defects which made for subjection, and struggled to the best of his ability to remove them. National dissensions have been a frequent cause of our repeated humiliation and subjection. He stood against them; he wanted to bring about the consolidation of our country. Though a devout Muslim whose work on the *Quran* has become a classic, he always stood for national unity and communal harmony. He made no difference between Hindu and Muslim, Sikh and Christain. He felt that all those who were in this country belonged to one country.

The national spirit was the driving force of his life. He was an apostle of national unity and communal harmony, the lessons which we have to remember even now as there are forces which are still at work in this country to divide us from one another, Indian unity cannot be taken for granted. It has to be nourished with great care in these days of linguistic and regional dissensions. These differences should be used to enrich the unity of India.

While his profound humanism is well known, he had a clear vision of what was right and what was wrong in public affairs. While he allowed compassion to sway his behaviour in personal relations, he never deviated from principles of justice so far as public affairs were concerned. He might forgive a man if he insulted him personally, but he who did a national disservice had to be dealt with adequately. Compassion in personal relations and justice in public affairs were his principles.

If we neglect probity in administration, the stability of the Government and the stability of our social structure will be undermined. He was much too fond of the right to prefer the wrong or the expedient. All along, whenever questions of administrative integrity arose, he fought for preserving high standards in public administration. That is another lesson which we have to remember.

Once freedom was won, he again felt that we must use that freedom for promoting social welfare, cleanse this country of sickness, squalor, illiteracy, and cleanse our minds of superstition, of obscurantism, of fanaticism. He stood for what one may call the emancipated mind, the min which is free from narrow prejudices of race or language, province or dialect, religion or caste. We had in Maulana Sahib the civilized mind.

Whenever I went to talk with him, he was full of quotations from Arabic and Persian. I do not know, but I was told that his command over these languages was unsurpassed and that the speeches which he gave in Urdu were firm in their structure, dignified and polished in their diction, and cogent and pointed in their purpose.

Let us remember that he worked for the ideals of national unity, probity in administration and economic progress. These are the things which we have set before ourselves. The only way in which we can honour his memory is for us to adopt these ideals and question ourselves every day, whether in our acts we are promoting national unity, we are promoting integrity in administration, we are promoting economic and material progress. That is the way in which we can imbibe the lessons of his life.

Books were his constant and unfailing companions. He wrote an *Introduction to History of Philosophy, Eastern and Western*, which began with a Persian couplet which compares the universe to an old manuscript of which the first and the last pages are lost. It is no longer possible to say how the book began nor do we know how it is likely to end.

To find out the meaning of life and existence is the purpose of philosophical quest. We may not succeed in finding it out but the pursuit of this quest is its own reward.

auyaktani bhutani vyaktamadhyani bharata
avyaktanidhananyeva tatra ka parivedana.

Maulana Azad ends the introduction with another Persian couplet which says: 'Those who follow this path never tire because it is both the way and the destination.' His life is an illustration of this. It was both the search and the attainment.

There is no doubt that we will not see the like of him again — a great man, a man of stately presence, indomitable courage and fearless behaviour.

Religion, Science and Culture
S. Radhakrishnan
Rs. 95.00

An inspiring and a masterly review of the various facets of religion and culture, and their application to life in the present day world.

'Dr. Radhakrishnan's sweep is as wide as the world, and wider.'

Tribune

'This book is not only meant to promote interpeople understanding but to awaken mankind to the danger of extinction of homo sapiens by nuclear destruction, the abyss it has reached by spiritual involution.'

Times of India

The Bhagvadgita

M.K. Gandhi   Rs. 80.00

In Mahatma Gandhi's own words his interpretation of the *Bhagvadgita* is designed for the common man — 'who has little or no literary equipment, who has neither the time nor the desire to read the *Gita* in the original, and yet who stands in need of its support.'

'Mahatma Gandhi's interpretation is unique by virtue of the simple style and illustrations from practical life...makes an interesting reading...'

Hindustan Times

'Designed for the common man who has no time or intellectual equipment to read the Gita in original...'

M.P. Chronicle

'I regard Gandhi as the only truly great... figure of our age.'

Albert Einstein

Hindu Dharma
M.K. Gandhi   Rs. 70.00

A critical interpretation by one of the greatest saints of the twentieth century.

'I do not consider myself fit to interpret Hinduism except through my own life...'

'I should reject it, if I found it inconsistent with my moral sense or my spiritual growth. On examination I have found it to be the most tolerant of all religions... Its freedom from dogma gives the votary the largest scope for self-expression. Not being an exclusive religion, it enables the followers not merely to respect all other religions, but to admire and assimilate whatever maybe good in other faiths. It is an evolutionary religion.'

Mahatma Gandhi

Dear Reader,

Welcome to the world of **Orient Paperbacks** — India's largest selling paperbacks in English. We hope you have enjoyed reading this book and would want to know more about books published by us.

There are more than 700 books on a variety of subjects to entertain and inform you. The list of authors published include, amongst others, distinguished and well-known names such as Arun Joshi, Anita Desai, Bhabani Bhattacharya, Dr. S. Radhakrishnan, R.K. Narayan, Mulk Raj Anand, John Buchanan, Shakuntala Devi, Khushwant Singh, Greg Chappell, Dr. O.P. Jaggi, H.K. Bakhru, Norman Vincent Peale, Robert Schuller, Windy Dryden and Paul Hauck **Orient Paperbacks** truly represent the best of Indian writing in English today.

We would be happy to keep you continuously informed of new titles and programmes through our monthly newsletter, **Orient Book Review**.

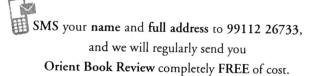

SMS your **name** and **full address** to 99112 26733, and we will regularly send you **Orient Book Review** completely **FREE** of cost.